THE SPIRIT OF MAN
IN ASIAN ART

THE SPIRIT OF MAN
IN ASIAN ART

Being the Charles Eliot Norton Lectures Delivered
in Harvard University 1933-34

by Laurence Binyon

C.H., D.Litt., LLD.

Late Keeper of Prints and Drawings in the British Museum

Dover Publications, Inc., New York

This Dover edition, first published in 1965, is an
unabridged and unaltered republication of the work
first published by Harvard University Press in 1936.
This edition is published by special arrangement
with Harvard University Press.

International Standard Book Number: 0-486-21435-4

Library of Congress Catalog Card No.: 65-24017

Manufactured in the United States of America

Dover Publications, Inc.
180 Varick Street
New York, N.Y. 10014

To

LANGDON WARNER

Preface

THESE lectures, when delivered to a general audience at Harvard in 1933–34, were illustrated by lantern-slides. It has not been found possible to illustrate them quite so fully in their printed form; but I hope that the illustrations here given will suffice the reader. For permission to reproduce paintings and sculpture which appear in this book I am indebted to owners both of public and private collections; to the authorities of the Boston Museum of Fine Arts, the Metropolitan Museum, New York, the Freer Gallery, Washington, the British Museum, the Victoria and Albert Museum, the Louvre, the Musée des Arts Décoratifs, the Berlin Museum, and the Bibliothèque Egyptienne, Cairo; also to H. E. H. the Nizano of Hyderabad, the editor of The Kokka, the directors of the Shimbi Shoin, Mrs. J. D. Rockefeller, Jr., Mr. Chester Beatty, Mr. Philip Hofer, and Mr. Charles Hoyt. I wish also to express my gratitude to those who during my stay in Cambridge helped me in so many ways with an inexhaustible kindness and courtesy; to the staff of the Fogg Museum, especially Mr. Edward Forbes, Professor Paul Sachs, and

Mr. Langdon Warner, the staff of the University Library, and the staff of the Harvard University Press. I am further indebted to Mr. Warner for invaluable assistance in connection with the illustrations to this volume.

L. B.

Contents

Lecture I

Lecture II

Lecture III

Lecture IV

Lecture V

Lecture VI

List of Illustrations

LIST OF ILLUSTRATIONS

THE SPIRIT OF MAN IN
ASIAN ART

Lecture I

INTRODUCTION

IN THESE lectures I propose to consider certain significant phases, certain pregnant moments, in the arts of the various countries of the continent of Asia.

I cannot of course attempt anything like a survey of the entire field; nor shall I approach the subject from an archaeological or historical or technical point of view. Rather I wish to show, if I can, — and I think this is more consonant with the object of the Professorship with which I have been honoured, — how the spirit of man, whether in China or India, in Persia or Japan, has expressed through creative art its relation to the world and to the universe; to suggest the likenesses and contrasts between these arts and the arts of Western countries, the reactions of the arts of the various races of Asia on each other, and the specific virtue in the contribution of each of them to the whole. Perhaps by the way we may be led to enquire into the nature of art itself.

At the present moment we in the West experience, and in experiencing resent, a consciousness of frustration. We have mastered and

3

harnessed the forces of nature for our own uses, but something, after all our efforts, eludes us. We have divided life into separate compartments, each presided over by a science with an imposing name; but the wholeness of life has somehow been obscured. What we seem to have lost is the art of living. I am inviting you to contemplate the creative achievements of another hemisphere, not only as an object of agreeable distraction, but also as something which may possibly suggest to us not unfruitful ideas on life and the art of living.

Looking on our world as it is, there are moments when one may be provoked to think that the most conspicuous characteristic of mankind is a gift for making a prodigious mess of its affairs, even, one might think, an unteachable stupidity, with all the cruelties directly and inevitably springing from that stupidity. But let us retain some faith in our kind. Behind this world-bewilderment, beneath the tangle of political and economic problems, lives still a spirit which, in spite of its capacity for folly and vileness, is delicate and sensitive, courageous and devoted. The best is hidden.

There is no history of human happiness. Of wars, plagues, and calamities; of crimes, con-

quests, and adventures; of enactments, of
voyages, inventions, and discoveries; of these
the pages of historians are full. But of the immense, silent, intangible life behind these re-
sounding efforts and events, how little, after all,
they tell us! And yet, if there is no written
history, there *is* a record of human happiness,
or rather of something intenser than happiness,
of human joy; the record is man's art. And
that record has one great advantage over the
history of historians: it is true. It is the expression of the spirit of man; and if it is false,
it betrays its own falsenesss; we are not de-
ceived. For we are so constituted that contemplating a work of creative art we can tell
just how finely or how coarsely organized was
the nature that conceived and wrought it. We
are aware of sincerity, and equally of insincerity.
The charlatan imposes for a moment, but no
more; infallibly he is found out.

The artist is inferior in one respect or another
to the gifted among his fellows: in the world of
action he is rarely at home, he may be unstable
and irresolute in his conduct, he may even be
incapable of sustained effort of intellect; but he
is more complete, because in him the life of the
senses, the life of the intellect, and the life of the

emotions combine into one. He thinks through feeling; and by imagination he can identify himself with natures outside his own. His creation comes from a stratum of being into which the conscious reason can never fully enter; and it is to a like stratum in our own nature that it appeals. There, our intuitions are at work, and their perceptions are more certain than our theoretic reasons. And since each man is a unique personality, different from everyone else, the artist's work is a sort of crystallization of his most secret and profound experience. So it is that when confronted with the art of races strange and foreign, even though we may know little of their history, language, and literature, we can with some sureness divine the temperament, the mental outlook, the attitude to life and to the universe, of these unknown artists. We can recognize the impress of a single personality, group his works together, and set beside them the works of his followers. We can recognize also the impress that every period leaves upon its own generation of artists. And as familiarity increases, we come to trace the swelling and subsiding of the waves of inspiration; we know when a certain spirit is present, and when it is absent; we know what one period

6

is capable of and another incapable; we are able at last to perceive order and continuity; we can date a given work within a definite epoch. We do this not by a process of reasoning so much as by a faculty within us, intimate as the sense of touch or taste. Every work of art is fragrant of its time.

Such a voyage of exploration among the arts of the East is fascinating in itself, for the new shapes and modes of beauty brought into our ken. But also it enables us to look back on the art and ideals of the West with a freshened vision, and perhaps to see them more truly. My experience is that when one arrives in the Far East, and one's thoughts turn back westward, all that Western civilization means to us assumes by contrast a more definite form and character than when one is in the midst of it.

If for a moment, then, we place ourselves outside that civilization in which we have grown up, we can better realize the rich complexity of the mental heritage which in daily life we take for granted. Greece, Rome, Judea — it is above all from these far fountain-heads that the streams flow to mingle in the modern Western mind. From Greece most of all. It is the Greeks who

7

determined the bent of the Western mind toward science, who set it on the unending road it journeys in the pursuit of truth for its own sake; the Greeks who to our vast good fortune gave us masterpieces of poetry on a grand scale such as no other early literature has approached; the Greeks whose philosophy coloured and shaped the conceptions of historic Christianity. The average man is hardly aware at all of the enormous debt he owes to that rich past, the fruits of which he uses and enjoys; that deep-rooted tradition of life and thought which stands so majestic in its continuity through all the turmoil of Western history. That ancient civilization of which we are the heirs is indeed a magnificent achievement of human reason. But it is not, as it has seemed for so many centuries, the only measure and standard by which we may judge of civilization. We can no longer inhabit it as a closed garden of the mind, believing that nothing outside it really matters. Our horizons have widened; the far has been brought near. And I feel that in the future when we speak of "the humanities" we shall have to incorporate in that conception not only the legacy of the Mediterranean world, but the contribution of Asia to the art and thought of mankind.

Some years ago I chanced to visit the house of a collector in London, and without preparation, after admiring the pictures, stepped from the modern house into a room designed and built by Inigo Jones, which the owner had bought entire and had had set up afresh as an adjunct to his house. It was not a very large room, but it seemed spacious, partly because of its loftiness, partly because it was empty of furniture, though panelled in wood throughout. It is strange how suddenly one can change one's mental climate. I seemed to have stepped straight into the seventeenth century; into England as it was when a plain majesty of style, the style of the Authorized Version of the Bible, came naturally to speech and pen, when also the glories of the Italian Renaissance were beginning to impress their forms upon art and architecture, as they had already coloured with flame the poetry and drama of England. It was like, I thought, inhabiting for a moment the mind of Milton; not of course the mind of Milton in the splendour of its activity, but in its receptive and quiescent state. Those simple yet stately proportions, that austerity of ornament, that disdain of the trivial which yet communicates no sense of emptiness but rather of latent richness

— these belonged to Milton's native air, to the time in which he lived.

One could hardly find, I think, a completer representative than Milton of that traditional Western civilization of which I have spoken. He belonged to a country in which much of barbarism still survived. He had all the fervour of the Northern Puritan. Yet he was saturated in every fibre by the inheritance of Greece and Rome. All his exquisite senses, all the artist in him, responded with spontaneous delight to the glories of the classic world.

Far more than most Europeans of his time, Milton was conscious of the world outside Europe. It is manifest that with his ardent curiosity of mind he had read all the books of travel that came his way; and had I the learning and skill of John Livingston Lowes, I might possibly be able to trace the pages that set his imagination on fire. He may have himself conversed with travellers from the East. Some actual experience must be reflected in similes like this:

> As when far off at sea a fleet descried
> Hangs in the clouds, by equinoctial winds
> Close-sailing from Bengala, or the isles
> Of Ternate and Tidore, whence merchants bring
> Their spicy drugs.

10

Was it merely for the sake of sonorous names
that roll upon the tongue,

> Damasco or Morocco or Trebizond,

that Milton loved to intersperse his epic with
these remote allusions? It was rather for the
vast horizons they evoked. He had the whole
cosmos distinct and mapped within his mind;
heaven and hell, and earth also. Looking West
he could see "the ocean barred at Darien";
looking South he could descry the peak of
Teneriffe lifting itself from the sea, and could
sail in thought beyond the Cape of Hope, past
Mozambique,

> to where northeast winds blow
> Sabaean odours from the spicy shores
> Of Araby the blest.

But it is the East that draws his imagination
most. He follows the flight of the vulture when,
leaving the haunts of Tartar nomads, he flies
toward the springs

> Of Ganges or Hydaspes, Indian streams,
> But on his way lights on the barren plains
> Of Sericana, where Chineses drive
> With sails and wind their cany wagons light.

He sees the snowy plains, where the Tartar retires before the Russian, or where the Persian

retires before the Turk; and that phrase which Wordsworth borrowed, "the gorgeous East," crystallizes the prevalent impression of the contemporary Moghul empire. But there is a touch of scorn in the "barbaric pearl and gold." And indeed from all these voyages of imagination Milton brings back no thought, only pictures. He has found in those far countries no lodge for mind or spirit. And even to-day, for most of us in the West, the continent of Asia remains picturesque and exotic, and awakens no response in the world of thought.

That great classic tradition, to the overpowering force of which a mind like Milton's so richly testifies, has lost, no doubt, in our day much of its old prestige; yet it exercises still a potent spell.

Anatole France was one day visiting the British Museum, and became eloquent in praise and enjoyment of the famous Greek marbles. When I offered to show him a Chinese statue of a Lohan, which had just been acquired but was not yet exhibited, he refused with decision. "No, no," he said. "The Greeks suffice me, I want nothing more; their art is perfect, its beauty is inexhaustible." And I do not doubt that had he seen the statue of the disciple of

Buddha, he would have turned away from that image of tense contemplation to even the remotest Roman copy of a Greek Aphrodite, parading her obvious charms. Such is the strength, the tenacity, of the classical tradition, which the French nation has cherished perhaps more exclusively than any other. But there is one other country in the world which has formed and fostered a tradition of art and life even more powerful and persistent and in the end even more exclusive; and that is China. Everywhere in Asia it is the art of China which, like Greek art in Europe, has enjoyed the greatest prestige. And the Chinese, at any rate since the Middle Ages, have tended to regard, and still regard, other nations, just as did the Greeks, as barbarians. Even Anatole France, had he confronted a representative of the old Chinese culture, would, very politely, have been made to understand that he was without the pale. Let us turn, then, to China.

Not far from Peking, between curves of the solitary hills, lie the tombs of the Ming dynasty. The Western visitor, told of imperial tombs, will surely expect some great and imposing structure, pillared and proudly ornamented, a structure meant to dominate its surroundings as the

dead emperors in life had dominated their subjects. But as he makes his way onward he finds
to his surprise no trace of human handiwork;
only as he penetrates further into the spacious
valley a sense of nature's vast peace deepens
upon him; and when, marking the approach to
the tombs, a single arch or gateway appears, it
is not that which impresses him, but the silent
amphitheatre of hills gradually becomes significant, as if part of an august design, and he
realizes that it is the hills themselves in their
solitude and grandeur that have been persuaded
to enfold this valley of the dead and to become
their "everlasting mansion." By submission
rather than compulsion the unknown architect
has conceived a sepulchre more enduring and
sublime than any man has ever built.

I think of that stately room of Inigo Jones's;
and it too seems a symbol, if only we complete
it with a garden, enclosed, well-ordered, with
turf soft to the feet, trees to shade the sun,
flowers to delight with scent and colour — a
piece of nature trimmed and subdued to human
pleasure. The bare and lofty room is a fit place
for the mind at home "in the spacious circuits of
her musing," as Milton puts it; the ordered
garden a place of solace and refreshment. Here

is nature mastered and put to service; here is
the mind within its fortress.

But in that far-away valley of Northern China
the mind goes out not in abstract speculation,
disdaining earth, but in serene reception. It
needs to pass no barriers. It has discovered a
harmony between its own life and the life of
nature; there is a flowing out and a flowing in.

Here is the keynote of the creative art of
China.

It was once supposed, and not so long ago,
for it is only in the present century that the real
achievements of Chinese art have been revealed
— it was once supposed that the art arose
under the stimulus of Buddhism. This is what
we might expect; because, in tracing the ripened
art of a gifted people to its beginnings, the art
of Italy for example, we are accustomed to find
that the first images it creates are inspired by
religion. Religion supplies the themes and at
first all is subordinate to the aim of assisting the
worshipper in his mood of devotion, of instruct-
ing him in doctrine, of edifying him with pictures of sacred story.

In China we find something different. The
earliest painting appears from records to have
been secular. In the bronzes and the jade im-

plements, which go back to a far remoter antiquity and which served for ritual purposes, we encounter animal forms that link the art of this race with the art of prehistoric man. The animal forms are not so much used for decorative purposes as incorporated into the shapes of ritual vessels. Behind this art with its grand design and imposing volume lies the art of the Asian nomads.

In the Eumorfopoulos collection there is a magnificent bronze incorporating the twin forms of sacrificial rams. In another collection is a bronze owl, and though the natural form seems to be entirely subdued to the shape of the vessel, splendid in its vigour and fullness, and though it is rather the idea of an owl than a representation of one, the challenging stare of the unblinking eye tells, in spite of the artist's rigorous convention, of something unsubduably alive. In some arts we find that animal or plant forms, originally well observed, have been used and repeated as decorative motives till all sense of the form as a living thing has been submerged and forgotten, and only a formula remains. That sort of degeneration is hardly known in China. The Chinese have kept their eyes fresh.

However the Chinese images of animals may be

transformed and conventionalized, as they often are — for a playful grotesqueness pleases these artists' fancy — they are creatures that have a life of their own; they are not a mere reflection of human suppositions and illusions about the life of animals.

The early bronzes are remarkable above all things for the sense of volume and power that they communicate, yet we note at the same time how springy are their curves. And I would say that what specially characterizes Chinese design throughout is a delight in movement as the manifestation of life. We see this especially when the artist is not creating a form in the round but is designing on a flat surface, whether painting, or incising on stone or lacquer, or modelling in low relief. At any rate from the Han period, at the beginning of the Christian era, Chinese designs have this character. The forms are full of animated motion, the lines run and flow.

This race has always had a turn for the fabulous, and it has imagined a number of fabulous animals, which, however fantastic, seem to have a credible existence; they are not like our heraldic animals, but are strangely alive. Chief among them is that superb creation, the Dragon.

17

I shall have more to say about the Dragon another day. Here we will note only that the Chinese passion for the idea of movement is so great that no creature of nature's making could satisfy it: it must needs invent a creature swift and sinuous as cloud or stream, a creature of infinite motion whose home is infinite space.

In an early fresco at Tun-huang [1] one sees horses which seem aspiring to dragonhood, as, prancing in air, they carry a saint over the tops of the mountains.

As we all know, the most ancient paintings and carvings in the world are of animals. Lying on their backs in the dim twilight of the caves they inhabited, Palaeolithic men drew and coloured vivid and powerful images of the wild beasts, the bison, the deer, the boar, which they hunted and killed in order to live. Imperious indeed seems the instinct for art in the human race. We are told that these paintings were made for magical purposes; they were thought to give men power over the beasts they hunted. But how could it occur to these primitive men that it was possible to work magic in this way, unless someone had first proved the possibility of making a picture? Surely the instinct to

[1] Photographed by the Fogg Art Museum expedition in 1924.

draw came first; but no sooner was it seen that drawings could be made than the priest-type of man would seek to put the artist-type in harness and make him and his art serve a general purpose. Art has always thus been persuaded to serve the uses of society; first, no doubt, for its supposed magical virtues, and later for its use in the service of religion.

As if this race cherished and preserved in a persistent memory its primeval experience, the Chinese seem to have carried with them from the remotest past into eras of civilization their early companionship with the world of animals. The men of the ancient Stone Age observed and studied the wild animals with the same passion and thoroughness that the Greeks and the artists of the Renaissance devoted to the human body. But the world of their perceptions was singularly limited. Life was to them an unending struggle between hunter and hunted. On that their gaze was fiercely concentrated, and nature to them meant the wild animals whose every movement they watched and noted, and nothing more.

All this concentrated observation is the first step made by man in his realization of the world around him. The animals are his enemies, but also his companions; he hunts them, but he admires their beauty and strength. In the primitive world these are the nearest existences to his own. They share with him delight in swift movement, the zest for life, the cunning in escape. But they are mysterious, they are voiceless; they are familiar, but also strange. They provoke him and entice him with hints of a beyond. They seem in their limitation of faculty below him, in their freedom and strength above him. They represent a world intermediate between him and the further, profounder, outlying mysteries of the universe.

In the art of Europe, before the nineteenth century, it seems as if man, intent on himself, on his own doings and aspirations, had lost touch with this life outside him. Intellectual curiosity rather than natural sympathy has led him slowly and gradually to study this intermediate world.

But the Chinese have never lost touch with that intermediate world of life; they have explored it more and more, not with the scientific curiosity of the European, but as if in a desire to be, so to speak, citizens of the universe, so that not only the beasts of the chase but the birds and the insects, and then beyond these the things we call inanimate, come to be included in their consciousness of the universal life.

This then is one thing that I would emphasize in Chinese art: its continuity with the primitive and its slowly widening and all-embracing sympathy with living things. It has its roots deep in the earth.

This continuity with the primitive has its other side. There is an absence of scientific curiosity, a temper of mind deliberately averse from the ardent enquiry into the nature of things which distinguished the Greeks. So in the popular mind belief in magic and all kinds of fanciful superstitions flourished exceedingly, and still flourish, side by side with an exquisite refinement and a consummate social wisdom. Childish as we may think these superstitions, there is a real poetry in that temper of mind which will not celebrate any normal event in life — birth, marriage, death, the building of a house, the sowing of the crops — without invoking the spirits supposed to dwell in earth and air, in the streams and the trees and the clouds. All nature is implored to be beneficent to the dawning life of the child, to the departing soul, as to every undertaking that is concerned with the tilling of the fruitful earth or helps to build the social fabric, centred in the life of the family. It is the credulous, popular side of what in the minds of poets, artists, and philosophers becomes a singular completeness of vision, a juster sense of man's place in the universe and of the relation of human life to the lives outside it than has ever prevailed in the West.

Confucius appears to have thought that the object of painting should be to preserve the edifying features of a great man. Unfortunately, of Chinese painting before the T'ang era (that is, the seventh to the tenth century after Christ) almost nothing has survived. Much the most important clue to the manner of this early period is the painting in the British Museum attributed to a famous master of the late fourth century. It may help to realize more vividly the unique continuity of Chinese civilization if we recall that Confucius was already in the fourth century as distant in the past as Dante from ourselves; and Confucius, of course, professed only to preserve and codify the wisdom of the ancients.

Let me first quote a little poem by a poet of the fourth century, because I think it will help us to understand the atmosphere, the mode of thought and way of looking at the world, out of

22

which the art flowered. The translation is
Arthur Waley's.

> Swiftly the years, beyond recall.
> Solemn the stillness of this fair morning.
> I will clothe myself in spring clothing
> And visit the slopes of the Eastern Hill.
> By the mountain-stream a mist hovers,
> Hovers a moment, and then scatters.
> There comes a wind blowing from the South
> That brushes the fields of new corn.

Attila had not yet scourged Europe with his
hordes, but the Roman Empire was majestically
crumbling in its long decay, when this poem was
written. How fresh it is, how sensitive! We can
see the hovering mist, we can feel the wind from
the South blowing on our faces. We note the
feeling of transience which makes the beautiful
moment more precious, also the touch of ceremony, the putting on of spring clothing to
be in harmony with the season. For ceremony
presides over Chinese life, and Confucius pre-
scribes a right way for the minutest detail of
behaviour.

Let us contemplate for a moment the painting
to which I have just referred. It is attributed to
Ku K'ai-chih, who flourished, as I said, in the
late fourth and the early fifth century. One of
the stories told about this artist is that a friend
borrowed some paintings from him, each rolled

up and kept in a box. The friend abstracted the pictures and returned the empty boxes. Ku K'ai-chih expressed neither suspicion nor surprise. "Paintings," he said, "partake of the nature of spirits. They have doubtless flown away to join the company of the immortals."

Here is a belief in magic, such as we associate only with primitive and backward races, yet it co-exists with a refined civilization, an art of living, such as few races have attained.

Anyone at all familiar with Chinese pictures and with the signatures of ancient and renowned masters attached with open-handed liberality to works of quite modern date, will understand that such an attribution as I have mentioned for the picture provokes immediate scepticism. Many and diverse judgments have been pronounced by the learned on this painting; but the Japanese scholars who have given it the longest and closest study, a study not of days but of months — scholars whose authority is unsurpassed in Japan — incline now to think that it cannot be later than the sixth century, and even say that there is just a possibility of its being an original. The general tendency, I think, has been to consider it a very early copy, whether of Ku K'ai-chih or another.

I am not surprised that those who have only seen it on a brief visit to the British Museum should have held a lower opinion of it than those who have devoted to it months of study; because to me, who have been familiar with it for nearly thirty years, it is infinitely more wonderful than when I first saw it. There are not too many works of art which continually gain and deepen for one in this way, and to this degree; certainly it is not an experience that one has with art of a secondary order. However, that is my experience in this case; and therefore I do not feel much concerned over the question of precise date or attribution.

The painting consists of a series of unconnected scenes, illustrating a little prose composition by an author of the third century, called "Admonitions of the Instructress in the Palace." The first two of these scenes, painted on the outermost part of the roll, have perished. The first of those which survive is the story of the lady Fēng, who, when a bear had broken loose at some games and was rushing toward the Emperor, threw herself in the animal's path. Her intended sacrifice was averted by two guards who ran up and killed it with their spears.

The second scene presents a lady of the first century before Christ who was invited by the Emperor to ride with him in his palanquin, but refused with a certain tartness. "No," she answered. "In the old pictures, wise and great princes have always illustrious ministers seated beside them; not favourites as in more degenerate days." In fact a favourite can be discerned seated beside the Emperor. This allusion to old paintings is one of a number of literary references from which we gather that it was mainly portraiture with which pictorial art began.

The series of figure-subjects is now interrupted by a landscape, or what seems to be a landscape; for it is really only a sort of symbol, though no doubt at this time landscape art was in a rudimentary stage. The text says: "In the eternal movement of the world there is nothing which is exalted that is not afterwards brought low. . . . When the sun has reached its zenith, it begins to sink; when the moon is full, it is on the way to wane. To rise to glory is as hard as to build a mountain out of grains of dust: to fall into calamity is as easy as the rebound of a tense spring."

The next is a toilet scene. A lady is having her hair done by a maid before a mirror, and another lady examines herself in her mirror. Beside them lies a lacquer box, with smaller boxes inside, the exact counterpart, even to the pattern on the lid, of a box found a few years ago by the Japanese in Korea and incised with a date of the first century. "Men and women know how to adorn their faces but there is none who knows how to adorn his soul. . . . Chasten your soul therefore; make it beautiful." So says the writing; but in the original at any rate one forgets the moral, one is lost in admiration of the subtle drawing of the turning wrist of the maid as she loops the heavy strand of hair, and the infinite discretion in her eyes. (Pl. 1.)

The next scene is a bedroom conversation, man and wife sitting in an alcove. Perfect trust, perfect frankness, is inculcated. And this is followed by a family group. The Emperor sits with certain of his wives and their children, one of whom is having his head shaved, while another is being taught by a tutor. "To utter a word seems an insignificant thing; but on it depends honour or shame. Think not to hide your thoughts; the heavenly mirror reflects not only what is visible. Say not that none has heard you: the Divine Ear has no need of sound. Be not vainglorious of your beauty; the mind of heaven loves not what is too complete. Confide not in your exalted rank; it is he that is highest who falls. . . . Let your hearts be all united as a swarm of locusts; so will you multiply your race."

Next we find a sage reproving a lady because she "seeks to charm with smiles put on." "No one can please forever. When love has reached its highest pitch, it changes its object; when it has reached its fullness, it fails not to diminish." The author in fact attempts a philosophic justification of polygamy. (Pl. 2.)

Lastly there is the Instructress, writing down her admonitions. Even in the photograph one can, I think, feel the delicacy and sureness of the brush-drawing. One notes too the undulating scarves, which give the feeling of an air blowing softly about the figures. It is part of that love of sinuous movement of which I spoke before. (Pl. 3.)

This painting is a precious testimony to Chinese conceptions of life. One must allow, of course, for the submissive position accorded to women, who are forbidden even to try to please forever. Evidently there were ladies who rebelled against these precepts, or the admonitions would not have been needed. But as a whole,

28

how humane is the atmosphere! What dignity and gentleness of manners it reflects! Certainly there is nothing here of the barbaric.

You will have remarked the insistence on the fact of mutability, and on the necessity of accepting that fact as inherent in our mortal lot.

Indeed, the paradox is that the marvellous stability of this civilization rests on its recognition and acceptance of change as the law of life. There is nothing of that defiant resistance to the natural processes of decay, that passionate assertion of the ego against the world, which has inspired the vast monuments built by great conquerors to endure, as they fondly thought, forever, and which has found eloquent expression in the art and poetry of Europe. There is no Byron crying that man is

> Triumphant when he dares defy;

nothing of that Renaissance mood of

> Is't not fine to dance and sing
> When the bells of death do ring?

In Western poetry mutability is a recurrent theme, a theme of lament over the passing of youth and strength and beauty, or of anger against the insulting blows of Time. A Greek poet speaks of old age as "hateful to boys and despised among women." Nothing could be in greater contrast with the Chinese reverence for age. Wordsworth indeed, who often reminds us of Chinese ways of thought, has expressed a serene acceptance of change in one of his finest sonnets:

> Truth fails not; but her outward forms that wear
> The longest date do melt like frosty rime,
> That in the morning whitened hill and plain
> And is no more; drop like the tower sublime
> Of yesterday, which royally did wear
> His crown of weeds, but could not ev'n sustain
> Some casual shout that broke the silent air
> Or the unimaginable touch of Time.

But with us such a note is, I think, exceptional.

Submission to the fact of mutability in a spirit of resignation is not, however, as we shall see later on, the attitude of the Chinese mind which most impresses; it is a sort of exultation, rather, in being a conscious part of the Protean life that streams and flows through all things.

Order alone, and obedience to order, will never wholly content the spirit of man. In that spirit there is the desire, often latent, often suppressed, yet still persistent, to transcend itself; to become different, to escape, to expand, to create. In a sense, it is what he is not which makes man what he is. This desire may take the form of a longing to escape from the trammelling conditions of daily existence; that is the romantic spirit, inspiring in the world of action adventure for adventure's sake, and in the world of imagination dreams of beauty: it dwells on the strange, the remote, the marvellous, the unattainable. Or it may take a more potent and more enduring form, and seek to pass out of its own limits and identify itself with other existences than its own, till it rises to become at last one with the universal spirit, the pervasive spirit of life.

And though at the core of Chinese life there is the wonderful stability and poise which we find reflected in that early painting, concentrated on human dignity and human responsibilities, yet Chinese art would not be what it is if this were all that it had to express and embody. Over this adjusted harmony of existence hovers a world of myth and legend, the world of the Rishi, the hermits, the mountain-dwellers who live on dew and have shed the grossness of mortality, so that their bodies have become immaterial and can float in air at will. Their paradise is an earthly paradise, yet partakes of the eternal. They are a sort of demigod, but not, like the demigods and Titans of Greek myth, rebels against the gods or against universal law. There are demons also, but these are represented with a certain playfulness, with no real terror; and the Rishi are happy and serene.

We are not surprised to find that the Confucian system, entering as it did into every detail of life and behaviour with a prescribed etiquette, proved to some natures, especially the poets and the artists, intolerably irksome. These preferred the way of the mountain-dwellers, the way of Lao-tzŭ, the great sage who was Confucius' rival. Hence a recoil to wilderness and solitude, a sudden flinging off of official cares and solemnities, a retreat to the free air of the mountains. Many were those who thus fled from the prison of office and social duty, and alone or with chosen companions passed their days by the mountain streams and among the bamboo groves; there they drank wine, made poetry and music, and cultivated the chrysanthemum. Here was no moroseness of the romantic egoist. These recluses were gay and happy. While Confucius was concerned with relating the laws of nature to human life and human order, they sought to relate their lives to the Pure Spirit pervading the universe.

Had Buddhism never brought its ecstasies into China, Chinese art would still, then, have

had this imaginative side. But one may conjecture that without other nourishment from
outside the imaginative art would have tended
to grow thin and tenuous. Buddhism, which
came into China in the early centuries of our
era, gave to art a whole new world of forms and
motives, and through these the art of China was
immensely enriched. With its quest of the Absolute, its promise of release from the cares of
the world and the sorrows of existence, Buddhism had enough affinity with the aspirations
of Taoism to make it easily acceptable. And it
brought from India not only conceptions of
greater grandeur, solemnity, and tenderness
than those of the Taoist world (which is paral-
leled rather in our conceptions of fairyland) —
it brought not only these, suffusing the Chinese
mind with a new fervour of emotion, but actual
works of sacred art.

Buddhist subjects were painted by Ku K'ai-
chih and by the other masters who worked before the T'ang period. These Buddhist paintings
have not survived, except for some wall-paintings at Tun-huang on the western frontier of
China. There is on the other hand abundance
of sculpture; but I will pass this early Buddhist
art by for the moment, being concerned rather

33

to show you a glimpse of the purely native Chinese style which was to assimilate so much from India, if only in the domain of religious art.

In the Boston Museum of Fine Arts is a precious scroll-painting, recently acquired, the "Thirteen Emperors," portraits painted by a very famous master of the seventh century, Yen Li-pen (Pl. 4). This may perhaps be an original. Here the types have changed; they are more massive and powerful, less slender and elegant. That is characteristic of the period. But it is only a variation on the same kind of painting as the roll attributed to Ku K'ai-chih. It is entirely free from Indian influence, which did not, at any rate directly, affect the secular art.

We usually think of China as jealously self-isolated and opposed to everything external to herself. Yet it was in the period of China's greatest creative energy and achievement, in material things as in art and poetry, that she opened her arms to this foreign influence and embraced this foreign faith. In this great T'ang period there was the liveliest curiosity about the Western countries; the long trade routes across the desert connected China with the Mediterranean; there was a come-and-go not only of merchandise but of thought and ideas and beliefs. With India especially there was full and fruitful intercourse both by land and by sea. Indian missionaries flocked into China, Chinese pilgrims into India. Indian sculptures were imitated and reverentially admired, as classic marbles were to be by the Italians of the fifteenth century.

Of all this I shall treat in my next lecture. We shall see how Indian thought and Indian art came to China as if predestined to complete the Chinese genius.

PLATE I

ADMONITIONS OF THE INSTRUCTRESS IN THE PALACE (detail), BY KU K'AI-CHIH.
CHINA, *ca.* 344–406 A.D.

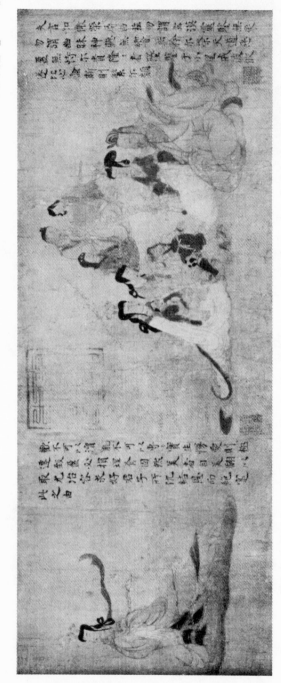

PLATE 2

ADMONITIONS OF THE INSTRUCTRESS IN THE PALACE (DETAIL), BY KU K'AI-CHIH. CHINA, *ca.* 344–406 A.D.

PLATE 3

ADMONITIONS OF THE INSTRUCTRESS IN THE PALACE (DETAIL), BY KU K'AI-CHIH. CHINA, *ca.* 344-406 A.D.

PLATE 4

THIRTEEN EMPERORS (DETAIL), ATTRIBUTED TO YEN LI-PEN. CHINA, *ca.* 640-680 A.D.

Lecture II

OKAKURA KAKUZO began his book *The Ideals of the East* with the challenging assertion, "Asia is one."

I have heard this assertion vigorously disputed. How can it be maintained that Asia forms anything like a unity, with its great diversity of races and religions? What is there in common between, say, Persia and Japan? How can such a unity be postulated when India, in especial, is so markedly different from the other countries of the Continent and is herself so divided by religious differences? The claim seems extravagant. Nevertheless we shall find that, in art at least, the countries of Asia have more in common than might be supposed. No Asiatic painting can be mistaken for a European painting. How is it that in all the countries of Asia the painters never, except where European influence has been at work, introduce the cast shadow or attempt to produce an illusion of natural effect? Common to all these countries, from Persia to Japan, is a felicity and vitality of line-drawing such as the West has scarcely ever, if ever, rivalled. These are not mere acci-

37

dents; they are symptoms of an attitude of mind; they tell of a mental attitude which cannot rest in the material world as an ultimate reality.

But besides this common mental attitude we are to trace currents of influence passing to and fro between the various countries, the wanderings of Ideas, those strangely potent, sometimes terrible essences that seize upon whole nations, to transform them. And this evening we will consider the impact of Indian thought and Indian art on the already maturing art of China.

The Indians, at least of Northern India, are of Aryan race. Yet how different are their way of thought and view of life from those of Europe! When Alexander invaded India, the naked ascetics, numerous then as now, excited his curiosity, and he questioned them through interpreters. They told him roundly that he was a nuisance to the world with his silly conquests; he had come all that way from his home only to plague himself and everyone else, and all of the earth that he would ever really possess would be what sufficed for a grave to cover his bones. Alexander, says the historian Arrian, "praised what they had said but continued to act in opposition to their advice." He could not, how-

ever, get them out of his thoughts; he wanted
to understand them. And when he came to
Taxila, he conceived a great desire that one of
them should live with him, because he admired
so much their singular patience and fortitude.
The most venerable of the ascetics dismissed
his invitation scornfully: if Alexander called
himself the Son of God, he was equally the Son
of God; there was nothing he desired that it was
in Alexander's power to give; he had all he
wanted, and when he died he would be delivered
from the irksome companionship of the body,
whereas Alexander and his men wandered about
and got no good from their wanderings. Nevertheless one of the ascetics, called Kalyana,
yielded; he gave up his way of life and joined
the Macedonians. Alexander made him his
friend. He went as far as Persia; but gradually
the alien mode of life so distressed and encum-
bered his spirit that he became ill and determined to die. Alexander sought in vain to
dissuade him, but at last reluctantly gave his
consent. A great pyre was built; and, with a
completeness of misunderstanding characteristic
of the West, Alexander thought to mitigate for
his friend the pangs of leaving this beautiful world
by ordering a profusion of precious things and

all kinds of incense to be thrown upon the pyre. There was a solemn procession; the whole army was paraded; trumpets were blown, and elephants added to the clamour with their plangent cries. But Kalyana, borne on a litter, paid no attention to these pomps intended in his honour; he gave away the rugs and bowls of silver and gold which were to have been consumed with him; he was happy again at last, and softly sang songs and hymns to the gods in his own language as he climbed the pyre and lay down on it. As the flames rushed over him, the Macedonians marvelled that he lay quite still and moved not at all. Alexander himself had withdrawn, unable to endure a sight so painful.

Truly it seemed that Oriental and European could find no point of contact. Yet these were of the same race by origin. The Chinese were of a totally different race from the Indians. Yet when Indian thought came to them with the missionary fervour of Buddhism, it took hold on the Chinese mind and came to permeate the empire. The greatest art of China is the art of the T'ang period, that is, from the seventh century to the tenth; and this was also the great period of Buddhist art.

But first let us see what sort of style the

40

Indian genius had formed in sculpture and painting.

The first period of Indian art culminates in the sculptures of the gateway of the great Stupa at Sanchi, which dates from the first century before Christ. This early Indian art is remarkable for its closeness to nature; animal forms, especially deer and elephants, are rendered with admirable truth to life. And though the Sanchi sculptures were ostensibly made in the service of Buddha, Dr. Coomaraswamy points out that "this art is not, as art, created or inspired by Buddhism, but is early Indian art adapted to edifying ends, and therewith retaining its own intrinsic qualities." So in the charming Dryad now in the British Museum (Pl. 5), leaning from her tree, we seem to be taken back to some primitive cult of the genial earth, associating so closely the ripe forms of the human body with the swelling growth of tree and bough.

We shall see how this poignant sensuousness came to be, not discarded in the maturer Buddhist art, nor opposed to spirituality, but reconciled with it.

That painting had been practised from very early times we know from literary references. In the most famous of classic Indian plays,

Sakuntala, there is a scene in which the hero contemplates a small portrait of Sakuntala, a miniature to be held in the hand. In another play of about the end of the sixth century there is a whole scene in which Rama and Sita contemplate and discuss a great wall-painting where scenes from their own life in the forest are depicted. Such painting on the walls of palaces had been an established practice for several centuries before this.

The earliest frescoes at Ajanta are supposed to date from the first century after Christ and the latest from about the sixth or seventh. They represent therefore the effort of many generations of artists, some more gifted than others, though there is a certain continuity of style in all. They are painted on the walls of temples or monastery halls carved out of the living rock of a great cliff which extends in a horseshoe curve over a stream below. This immense series of paintings holds the central place in the pictorial art of Asia.

The paramount impression is one of abounding, exuberant vitality. The compositions are not enclosed in definite framing borders, but merge into one another. There is an astounding variety of forms, postures, gestures. Accustomed as we are in Western art to the elaborate devices of painters to secure a decorative unity in large-scale compositions, the attitude and movements of forms and groups being dictated by the desire for harmony and symmetry, we may be sometimes disconcerted by the relative absence of what is called the logic of design. These artists are inspired rather by faith in the unity of all life, not of human beings only, but of all creatures — insects, animals, flowers and trees, men and women, deities and angels. The sense of that unity underlies all their creations. And though at first we may be prompted to crave for a more obvious and reasoned coherence in the compositions, yet when we turn back to such typical Western masterpieces as, say, Raphael's frescoes in the Stanze of the Vatican, there in turn we shall miss the joyous ease of casual movement, the natural grace which we can discover in a group of children at play, and which unites the apparent diffuseness of the Ajanta paintings: we may feel something too much of calculated arrangement, something too much of the conscious and imposed, in the admirable design.

At Ajanta all seems spontaneous and instinctive, though no doubt there is conscious art at

work. Something is due to a difference in the
actual mould of the human forms; to the pliancy
and gentleness of limbs which are not powerful
and muscular, but graceful, lithe, and active;
still more to a difference of method and practice.
Here are no posed models, separately studied
and then fitted into their places in the composition. The Indian artist would paint from
memory, but a memory severely trained by
watching the natural movements of the body,
especially in the movements of the dance. And
he would have one great advantage over the
European artist in that the unclothed body seen
in the fields or on the highway in all the daily
occupations of life was to him familiar from infancy. Hence the singular felicity in drawing
human forms in movement or repose.

The landscape background, such as it is, is
tentative and grasped in details rather than as
a whole. Yet there is a pervasive sympathy with
the life of animals and birds, and trees and
flowers: a sort of warmth and glow in the vision
of life on the fruitful earth, — men, women, and
children, out of doors among the springing
plants and trees or in the porticoes of palaces
or at city gates; but always mingled with these
is the presence of a spiritual element, whether

44

manifested in transcendent forms or appre-
hended as something latent but very real.

We must remember what filled the minds of
these Indian artists. They were called on to
illustrate the life of the Buddha; not only his
incarnation as Gotama, the prince who became
the Enlightened One, but the previous incarnations in which he appeared, now as a deer, now
as a goose, now as an elephant, now as a man.
In each incarnation he manifests the same gentleness, the same selflessness. So it is a vision
of the spirit passing successively through all
forms of life, acquainted with the sorrows of
them all, and emerging with infinite charity and
compassion in man; this is the vision before
these painters' eyes, this the theme which unites
every scene they picture.

The consummation of the art of Ajanta is
seen in the great figure of Padmapani, the Bodhisattva who performs the duty of the Buddha
since the disappearance of Gotama, till Mai-
treya, the Buddha who is to come, descends to
earth (Pl. 6). The Bodhisattva appears as a
young prince of noble birth and breeding, with
his consort beside him: it is as if the whole world
were in his eyes, and he looks down on it in
boundless compassion. This graceful but ma-

45

jestic form is not detached from the teeming earth, not throned apart, but seems to emerge from the intricate, varied life of man and nature: he holds all our gaze at first, and only by degrees do we become conscious of other forms: a woman leaning on her lover's shoulder, peafowl gleaming blue from sombre foliage, monkeys at play, and in the air the floating shapes of supernatural beings.

Different from this, of simpler majesty, more aloof but full of the same tenderness, is the figure of the glorified Buddha returning to his native city and asking alms of his wife and child. This fresco is, I believe, very difficult to see in the cave where it is painted. The original is on a great scale, and though damaged, like all these paintings, must be profoundly impressive.

The actual character of the art of Ajanta at its finest may best be seen in a detail on a larger scale, such as the head of a princess, to whom lotus flowers are being offered (Pl. 7). The work of this unknown artist seems to belong to the ripest period of Ajanta painting. The ease and mastery of the brushwork are astonishing. The painter seems as if unaware of difficulties. It is like a natural eloquence. And yet there is no callousness such as so often, in a ripe art, comes with the pleasures of mastery. It is profoundly sensitive. There is not the least consciousness of any spectator in this thoughtful face, telling of rich capacities of emotion and understanding.

You will notice something very rare in Eastern art, the sense of relief and roundness, emphasized by reticent high lights on salient features and a suggestion of modelling.

This plastic sense is still more apparent in the frescoes of Bagh. Bagh is in Gwalior State; and the rock-hewn caves there once contained an extensive series of frescoes, of which only a small portion remains. These and some paintings on a rock in Ceylon are almost all that have survived besides those at Ajanta; but no doubt many more series of frescoes at other sites have perished from the climate or been destroyed by Muhammadan iconoclasts.

What has survived at Bagh is the representation of a festival and the procession of people going to it on horseback, on elephants, or on foot. Dancers are surrounded by circles of girl musicians. It may seem a strange embellishment of a monastery wall. But in India religion is not something set apart from daily life, but inseparable from existence as the perfume from

47

the flower. And I suppose the Buddha's universal charity, his rejection of the austerities practised by the ascetics, would create an atmosphere congenial to the painter's normal delight in picturing living things. (Pl. 8.)

The Bagh frescoes are much less famous than those of Ajanta; but they seem to me if anything superior, as art. We are amazed by the mastery of form and movement, because the mastery seems not to come from laborious study and obedience to rules but to be (so to speak) a flowering of the mind in form. It is true that there are in the paintings which survive no such sublime conceptions as we find at Ajanta; but there is a greater rhythmical felicity in the discovery of the beauty inherent in natural gesture and attitude. Above all, there is a perfect fusion of the sensuous and the spiritual. The spiritual significance of life is not emphasized so as to become disdainful of the lovely body and the warm earth; it is felt rather as something which pervades and perfumes all that breathes, like the light touch of wind blowing from we know not where; something which unites and does not divide.

This natural poise and harmony seem to be the active power which animates the glowing scenes, making what are called aesthetic necessities appear as almost irrelevant externality. The colour is deep and ardent: the blue and white stripes of the scant garments foil the dark richness of the supple bodies.

In the elephant procession we are struck by something still more removed from primitive art; for here there is pictured a movement not merely across the space before the spectator but obliquely from the background towards the front. The sense of motion is emphasized, too, by the suggestion of swaying movement in the elephants' riders. We feel the slow ponderous advance of the huge animals. These paintings, which without their colour may appear a little confusing at first sight, can hold their own with any pictorial art in the world. But like the maturer art of Ajanta they present a curious problem. There is nothing like them in later Indian art, which is flat and in two dimensions. Yet they are absolutely Indian in character. The plastic element which we have noticed might seem to betray an affinity with Mediterranean art; and Greek influence has been supposed by some writers. Essentially, it seems to me, the relation is more with early Indian sculpture, such as the Sanchi Dryad which I showed a little while ago. There is the same seizure of living form, the same feeling of exuberance.

Yet the problem remains. Why was this expression of plastic feeling not developed in later painting? In any case we must note it as something exceptional in Asia, where pictorial art relies on line for the suggestion of the form it encloses. We find indeed that in Chinese Turkestan and also in Japan occasional examples of Buddhist painting show a tentative system of modelling in half-tones, but it is a foreign element, not really understood, and is on the way to becoming merely a decorative convention. The problem remains; and if there is a solution, I have failed to find it.

That there is a Greek influence in the Buddhist art of the Farther East is of course undeniable. But this word "influence" is often much abused. With every creative artist, the more aglow with inspiration he is, the more open is he to absorb from any and every source that will feed his mind, but, whatever it may be, he will absorb it and make it his own. So it is with races. We must distinguish, and note what is the dominant element, what is merely an ingredient. Professor Strzygowski has discovered a curious convention for the representation of

mountain-forms, like the débris of masonry, oc-
curring in mosaics at Ravenna, at Ajanta, and
in early paintings in Japan. These may indicate
(as he contends) a common origin; but such
things as these are conveniences which an artist
may borrow because he finds them useful; they
are not things that fire his soul and enlarge his
imagination. These are the influences that are
really interesting, when spirit meets spirit. It
is the Indian influence on Chinese art, not the
Greek, which was stimulating and inspiring.

Buddhism and Buddhist art came first to
China by way of Peshawar, Afghanistan, and
Central Asia.

About the beginning of the Christian era a
tribe which occupied part of North-west China
were driven out of their territory and, moving
south, occupied the country then known as
Gandhara, that is, part of Afghanistan and part
of the Panjab; later they advanced their rule
still further into India. In Gandhara arose a
prolific art which, though put to the service of
Buddhism, was the work of Hellenistic crafts-
men, continuing presumably traditions surviving in the little kingdoms set up after Alexander's
conquests. The result was an art of mixed elements. Some scholars, possessed by the prestige

of everything Greek, have insisted on the Hellenistic elements and have supposed that this late
Mediterranean tradition exercised a formative
influence on the art of China and Japan. The
dating of these sculptures is problematical, and
controversy has raged over the question whether
the Buddha type (for some centuries the representation of Buddha was reverentially avoided)
was first created in Gandhara or in India itself.
With this question we need not be concerned.
What we shall note is rather that the types taken
over from images of Greek deities became more
and more Indianized. And this is only what
we should expect. The interior conception is a
more potent and vital thing than the exterior
craftsmanship. What Gandhara gave to the art
of the Farther East was a certain convention,
which has its Western parallel in the general
convention of types and dress prescribed by
tradition for the figures of Christ and his
apostles. For just as to European painters
those sacred figures could only be imagined —
they had no idea of the actual features or dress
— so the Chinese adopted conventions of types
and draperies from the Gandharan school; but
the spirit within the forms was their own, and
new.

What could be more different in essence from Graeco-Roman art, with its ideal of purely physical beauty, than the sculpture of the Wei dynasty in China? The Wei were a tribe of nomads from the North who conquered part of China and eagerly sought to adopt the Chinese culture. But, as Mr. Yetts in his masterly essay on the evolution of Buddhist art in China has argued, the art now associated with the Wei probably owed nothing to this bloodthirsty invading tribe but was essentially a Chinese style.

After that brief glimpse of Buddhist painting in India, let us return to China. When in the seventh century we come to the T'ang period, we find Buddhism firmly established in China and inspiring the grandest art of the period. Then, as never before or since, intercourse between India and China, not only by land, through the Western extension of the Chinese Empire, but also by sea, was full and frequent. There were thousands of Indian monks in China, and innumerable pilgrims, some of whose records are extant, made the long journey to the Holy Land of India and brought back sacred images, and sacred scriptures which were translated into Chinese.

How direct at this period was the influence of

Indian art on Chinese may be illustrated by an
example. There is a beautiful torso in the India
Museum in London which is a work of the classic
Gupta period. Compare with that the splendid
Chinese statue of the T'ang period in the collection of Mrs. Rockefeller in New York (Pls. 10
and 11).

It was not now a mere borrowing of superficial
features; it was a fructifying contact with the
greatest art that India had produced. China,
possessing already a great art of her own, assimilated readily the inspiration of Buddhist ideals,
although the secular art, as we saw last week,
remained true to native traditions. The eighth
century saw the climax of China's military expansion westward; Ch'ang-an, the capital, was
a world-centre where not only Indians but
Persians, Turks, and Syrians met; Manichaeism, Zoroastrianism, and Christianity were practised side by side with Buddhism.

It was a period of splendid achievement, of the
greatest poets (according to general estimation)
and the greatest painters that China has ever
produced, though of the painting very little has
survived.

The China of this period presents an aspect
strangely contrasting with the self-enclosed

China of later times. We know how richly
creative and original genius — Shakespeare for
example — is ready to borrow freely from external sources, where minds less rich would be
too scrupulous. China now borrowed decorative motives from Persia and from Hellenistic
art, just as she welcomed foreign painters; but
whatever she took she speedily absorbed.

We may wonder perhaps that the people of
a great and wealthy empire, which had carried
its victorious arms so far across Western Asia, a
people conscious of creative vigour, expressed in
virile art, should have embraced so fervently
the Buddha's gospel of Renunciation. But
Buddhism was no longer the simple ethical doctrine of its founder; it was a complex system
which admitted various schools of thought. Its
development on the philosophic side appealed
to the Chinese intellectuals. These were comparatively few, no doubt; but on the human
side it appealed to the common people as a
promised refuge and relief from the troubles of
existence. The Western conquests of the Empire were achieved at the cost of immense
misery; and Chinese poetry is full of the laments
of those who were compelled to take service in
the dreadful desert, defending the Great Wall,

and returned home in old age only to die. We need not wonder at the success of Buddhism in Asia more than at the success of Christianity in Europe: the rulers of Christian countries have not been remarkable for avoiding battle and bloodshed in the pursuit of their ambitions.

A glimpse of Chinese life under the T'ang dynasty has been revealed to us, in one aspect of its secular art, during the present century, through the opening of tombs of the period and the discovery of the pottery figures now familiar in the West. These figures represent the households of important people, sacrificed in primitive times at the death of a chieftain, as we have seen in the recent excavations at Ur of the Chaldees, till humaner views substituted images for living beings. Though the work of artisans, they show a superb vigour and animation. We see cavalcades of horsemen, camels with their grooms, ladies, attendants, dancers, actors, musicians. Complete contents of tombs are to be seen only in the Toronto Museum, but groups and scattered figures are in many museums and private collections. The horses and camels, modelled with a noble naturalism, are particularly splendid. The Chinese seem to have had a passion for fine horses, and emperors would wage costly and devastating wars in order to get horses of the breeds for which some Central Asian countries, such as Ferghana, were famous. Tribute from vassal kingdoms in the West often came in the form of horses. At one time there were forty thousand in the imperial stables. They were the favourite subject of one of the great T'ang painters, Han Kan. It was as a symbol of speed and beauty of movement that the horse was so admired; it was often pictured in its free life on the plains, rejoicing in its strength and swiftness.

Even in this art of the potters we can see what power, what animation, was in the native, the secular Chinese tradition. Unfortunately almost nothing has survived of eighth-century painting by the great masters. Yet we know that Wu Tao-tzŭ, the greatest of them all, devoted himself mainly to Buddhist themes. He painted three hundred frescoes on monastery walls, but these have perished; most of them, if not all, were destroyed later in the century at a time when a reaction against foreign ways and the foreign religion was for the moment triumphant and a wholesale destruction of Buddhist art was decreed.

For a glimpse of what Buddhist painting was

like in the T'ang period we must turn to the discoveries made at Tun-huang in 1907. Tun-
huang is a city on the western frontier of China.
It was an important place; for here started the
chain of oases which made possible the danger-
ous journey across the Great Desert. It was
the gate through which passed all those elements
of Indian, Persian, and Mediterranean civilization which trade and missionary religion alike
brought into China. Near Tun-huang is a rock-
wall hollowed into shrines, and filled with
sculpture and frescoes, some of them dating
from the fifth century. Some remarkable fragments of frescoes are in the Fogg Art Museum.
In one of these shrines, in a walled-up library,
Sir Aurel Stein found thousands of manuscripts
and hundreds of paintings on silk, some of the
latter bearing dates of the ninth and tenth
centuries.

It would seem likely that Buddhism was first
preached orally in China; for in some of the
small paintings at Tun-huang, where the Buddha legend is depicted, we find that not only
the buildings but the figures, even Buddha himself, are Chinese — as if the artists had never
seen any Indian or Gandharan images or paintings but pictured the scenes as happening in

China. But as soon as such images were introduced Buddhas and Bodhisattvas were imitated from imported examples.

But legends of the life of the historic Buddha or of his previous incarnations are not the staple theme of Chinese Buddhist art, which is concerned rather with other Buddhas and with the Bodhisattvas. For even in India Buddhism had developed into something very different from its primitive simplicity, and in its long journey across Asia it seems to have absorbed elements from other religions, and had become a very complex system, which in China and Japan was to pass through many phases and divide into a number of different sects. The main thing for us to notice is that emphasis has passed from the ideal of personal salvation to the ideal of the salvation of the whole world.

What is a Bodhisattva? A Bodhisattva is a human being who, having passed through successive stages of existence, and perfected himself, so that he has earned the right to enter Nirvana, renounces that bliss till the salvation of the whole world be accomplished. The Bodhisattvas therefore became favourite objects of worship and prayer, especially Avalokitesvara, or Kuanyin as he is called in China, the genius

59

of Compassion, who is said to hear the cry of every sentient thing.

Just as we saw how in primitive times the imagination of man had been possessed by the animal world, outside itself yet living, which formed a link between its own consciousness and the mystery of the world beyond, so now, at a later stage, it creates an intermediate world of beings between the so finite human soul in its weakness and the Infinite, the Imperishable, the Absolute.

Kuanyin is the spiritual son of Amitabha Buddha, the Lord of Boundless Light, who presides over the Western Paradise. There the souls of the blessed are born in the lotus buds that spring from the lake; and above are pavilions, peopled by beatified spirits, for whom celestial music is forever played, and the celestial dancer forever dances in their midst.

Many are the pictures of Paradise found at Tun-huang. Some of these are most elaborate compositions, crowded with figures in the Indian manner of design; yet with all their intricacy there is no sense of confusion, there is on the contrary a sense of abounding peace. The Chinese gift for creating harmony by a continuous relation between the forms is subtly exerted to control the multitude of figures into an ordered whole.

The character of these compositions can be seen even in details (Pls. 12 and 14). There is not the sort of seeming accident, the suggestion of seething life overflowing its boundaries, that we find in many early Indian paintings and reliefs. The latent rhythms have become more visible, more emphasized. But there is as yet no freezing of the forms into a hieratic convention. These heavenly beings are not the richly sensuous forms that we saw in India. They are remoter, more ethereal; but they too are living, they give one the persuasion of being individual persons, with their gracious movements and gestures.

How natural is the pose of the celestial nymph seated at the upper window of a pavilion! The type is Indian, but with a difference. And how beautiful is the design of the tree with its broad leaves of pale green, foiled by the blue-gray of the roof, and the vermilion of the pillars! (Pl. 14.)

These two illustrations are from the same picture, the finest of all the Tun-huang silk-paintings. This, one feels, is painted by an artist, whereas the majority are painted rather

61

by artisans. The variety of style is remarkable. While some are purely Chinese, many are in a mixed style, the work of painters from Turkestan, further west.

The difference is readily discernible. The tendency as we move westward is to emphasize what is solid, what is stable: the tendency of China, of the Farther East, to dwell on what is floating, undulating, airy. The seated Bodhisattva reproduced on Plate 13 — it is Khsitigarbha, the Pilgrim who knocks upon the doors of Hell and brings light in his flaming jewel to the dwellers in its pains — this seated figure may be said to be Chinese in general convention, but it betrays its affinity with the West by a certain solidity of pose. The form is firmly planted, static; the flowers seem pinned in their place. At any rate the difference is manifest when we compare it with the standing Kuanyin on the same plate. The Indian type is still there, with its rather heavy forms, but it has undergone a transformation which has suppled the form and made it pliant. The skirt is a vivid orange-red, contrasting with the emerald green of the scarf. It has the character of an apparition from the darkness, and looks as if it obeyed other laws than those which obtain on the gross earth. The floating scarf undulates in the motion of a gentle wind, like the sinuous lines of incense smoke rising and floating on the air. Flowers fall delicate and tremulous; they seem to glide before our eyes.

In looking at these paintings, brought to light after a thousand years of lying in darkness and oblivion, you must remember that they are provincial works only. They are mere echoes of the work of the great masters.

It is strange how the Chinese, a race famed for their practical wisdom, their generally mundane temper, had the gift, in interpreting a foreign religion, of communicating spiritual conceptions with such immediate directness through their art.

Were they perhaps helped by the fact that Buddhism was a foreign religion? that those gracious presences which they sought to evoke, those incarnations of Boundless Power, Boundless Wisdom, Boundless Compassion, were already for them remote from the actual world of life? that they were not conceived, as the Indian artists conceived them, in terms of the humanity around them, familiar to their eyes from infancy, but were already distant in the world of the spirit? No doubt, when we recall

63

the great Bodhisattva at Ajanta, surrounded by earthly forms and the green growths of earth — a human shape in which we can feel the pulsation of the blood beneath the skin — something seems to be lost. We turn to the creations of the Chinese painters, and the reality of the forms is diminished. To the Chinese worshipper even the type of countenance, the mould of bodily shape, no less than the folds and adjustments of the dress, would be strange and different from anything he saw in his own life. These Bodhisattvas would come to him as visions from the unknown.

But this is not all the difference. The Chinese native art, before the coming of Buddhism, had shown a unique gift for communicating the sense of immaterial forms floating in space; and the Chinese imagination had long been familiar with the mountain-dwellers, the solitaries, who living a life of contemplation, and attenuating the needs of the body to the farthest point, have glided into immortality. For the tracing of airy movement the Chinese writing-brush was an unrivalled instrument; and now it was to be used to evoke the presence of gracious beings removed from all accident of earthly existence and conceived as possessing in unbounded

64

measure the courage, wisdom, and compassion which man feels within himself but cannot in life attain.

There is a fresco of three Bodhisattvas about twelve feet square, in the British Museum (Pl. 15). It seems strange that forms so massive should appear so immaterial. For all their assured stability and profound peace they seem to have a latent floating movement, and the scarves they wear sway slowly as weeds trail in a stream. Over all is a flush of ethereal colour.

There is no longer the wonderful equilibrium of spirit and sense which we found at Bagh and at Ajanta. We have passed over, into a world beyond this world. Perhaps it is only natural that the Chinese, a people so deeply attached to the earth and earthly things, should, when they seek to evoke spiritual presences, intensify their unearthliness. For them the spiritual element is not, as with the Indians, something invisibly pervading, and inseparably belonging to, human life.

This fresco, majestic as it is, represents a comparatively late stage in the Buddhist tradition of China. It is perhaps four centuries later than Wu Tao-tzŭ, the supreme master; and, doubtless, could any of his perished works be restored to us, this would seem but an echo of eighth-century grandeur. We have records and descriptions of Wu Tao-tzǔ's godlike power as he swept his great forms upon the wall. It is told that his figures were like sculpture, that they "seemed to walk out of the picture and back into it."

But almost the only certain works of the eighth century now surviving are a small series of portraits of saints now at Kyoto. I reproduce the best preserved of the series (Pl. 16). The painter of it had no great fame, and we may suppose it to be a typical, though not outstanding, specimen of eighth-century painting. Yet I think we feel at once that it belongs to a great period. Just as there are no flourishes of calligraphy in the brush drawing, so there is a great sincerity in the portraiture of this old priest. The original painting is very moving. There is an unusual solidity in the figure, and one may suppose that Wu Tao-tzǔ could communicate this sense of solidity in a far higher degree.

In fact, a certain massiveness seems to have characterized all the art of the T'ang period. Perhaps the heavier forms of Indian Buddhist art affected the Chinese style; that is, in religious painting. But I think this greater solidity, which is felt not only in Buddhist art, may betray also some imponderable influence from the West. For this period was the one in which China accepted and welcomed foreigners from the countries of Western Asia as far as the Mediterranean, and was herself induced to pursue an aim of material aggrandisement.

What, in sum, are we to say of this potent wave of Indian thought and art which passed over China in this fruitful period? It is no case like that of Gandhara, producing a hybrid art, the elements of which can easily be separated in the mind. Let us remember rather how Rubens transformed the Northern traditions he inherited by assimilating the fluent rhythms and grand style of Italy: he retained his native outlook, but created a new style entirely his own. So it was, I believe, with Wu Tao-tzŭ, though the character of the transformation was so different. Indian Buddhist art has one beauty, Chinese Buddhist art another.

But while the Buddhist art of India came to an end even while passing on its conceptions to China, and Buddhism itself died out in the land of its birth, both the religion and its art, enriched by the contact with Chinese genius, travelled on yet further to Korea and Japan.

67

We shall see later what a stimulus and enrichment this was to Japanese art and to the world's inheritance of beauty. But next week we will continue the consideration of Chinese art, and in especial the landscape painting.

PLATE 5

STONE DRYAD, FROM THE GREAT STUPA AT SANCHI.
INDIA, 1ST CENTURY B.C.

PLATE 6

PADMAPANI. WALL PAINTING AT AJANTA. INDIA, LATE GUPTA PERIOD

PLATE 7

HEAD OF A PRINCESS. WALL PAINTING AT AJANTA. INDIA, LATE GUPTA PERIOD

PLATE 8

GIRL MUSICIANS. WALL PAINTING IN THE BAGH CAVES. INDIA,
LATE GUPTA PERIOD

PLATE 9

STONE BODHISATTVA AT THE YÜN KANG GROTTOS. CHINA, 5TH CENTURY

PLATE 10

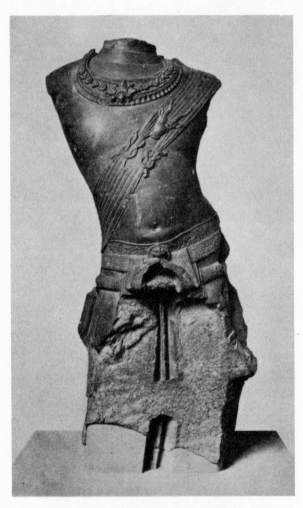

STONE TORSO OF AN INDIAN PRINCE.
GUPTA PERIOD

PLATE **II**

STONE BODHISATTVA. CHINA, T'ANG DYNASTY

PLATE 12

DETAIL OF A PARADISE SCENE, FROM THE TUN HUANG GROTTOS.
CHINA, T'ANG DYNASTY

PLATE 13

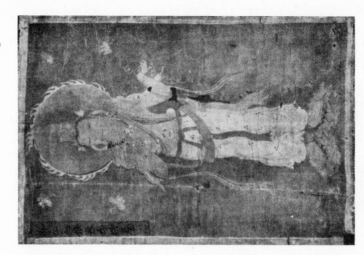

AVALOKITESVARA, FROM THE TUN HUANG
GROTTOS. CHINA, T'ANG DYNASTY

KHSITIGARBHA SEATED, FROM THE TUN HUANG
GROTTOS. CHINA, T'ANG DYNASTY

PLATE 14

DETAIL OF A PARADISE SCENE, FROM THE TUN HUANG GROTTOS.
CHINA, T'ANG DYNASTY

PLATE 15

THREE BODHISATTVAS. WALL PAINTING. CHINA, *ca.* 12TH CENTURY

PLATE 16

BUDDHIST PATRIARCH, ATTRIBUTED TO LI CHEN.
CHINA, 8TH CENTURY

Lecture III

SHELLEY, walking in the woods near Florence, watched the approach of a great autumnal storm. And watching it he was moved to write an impassioned invocation to the unseen presence of the West Wind:

> Wild Spirit, which art moving everywhere;
> Destroyer and preserver; hear, O hear!

He sees the menace of its "congregated might of vapours," about to burst in "black rain, and fire, and hail," and the long tresses of streaming cloud remind him of a fierce Maenad. Yet in spite of its power of destruction, felt even in the oozy bottom of the sea, he longs to share in the wind's "skiey speed," even if only as "a wave, a leaf, a cloud," lifted upon its elemental motion.

The West Wind was to Shelley a symbol. But for the European mind there was no symbolic image at hand of universal import which could embody his conception. Shelley's memory was stored with the myths of the Greek imagination; and the image of the Maenad, possessed with Bacchic frenzy, comes to his mind, but it is not great enough to fill it.

69

The well-known Southern Indian bronze images of Nataraja may seem at first sight far removed indeed from our world and from Shelley's poem. Yet in essence the idea embodied in the bronze is the same, or near akin to it. It is Siva, the Destroyer and Preserver, dancing the dance of Creation (Pl. 17). He tramples a demon under his foot, and the energy of his being overflows into an aureole of leaping flames. "Like the heat latent in firewood," he is said to diffuse his power in mind and matter and make them dance in their turn. We in the West have through the patient investigations of science arrived at a similar conception of an eternal Energy as the reality behind appearances. But as yet this remains rather a private possession of men of science; it has not become ingrained in our habits of thought. Nor have we any image to embody it in art. It is characteristic of India that this conception should be embodied in the form of a god. But to the Chinese, so much more free from anthropomorphic tendencies, this would have been too definite, too human a symbol. If Shelley had been a Chinese poet, his ode would inevitably have been addressed to the Dragon.

What is it that the Dragon symbolizes? We

have seen how the Chinese mind and Chinese art assimilated Indian religious conceptions and religious imagery brought by Buddhism. It was a fruitful impregnation, it provided a new field of plastic and pictorial motives, it gave a glow of emotional fervour. But it did not by any means fundamentally alter the course of Chinese art, or submerge the native traditions. Buddhism could not have appealed to the Chinese mind if China had not already developed ideas of a kindred order: I mean the ideas associated with Lao-tzŭ and his followers.

"The Tao which can be expressed in words is not the eternal Tao; the name which can be uttered is not its eternal name. . . . Only one who is eternally free from earthly passions can apprehend its spiritual essence; he who is ever clogged by passions can see no more than its outer form." [1] So begins the little book which contains the sayings of Lao-tsŭ; sayings paradoxical, sometimes difficult and obscure, but always pregnant and stimulating. To read these brief pages is like breathing mountain air.

What is Tao? It means The Way, and has been variously interpreted.

[1] The quotations given are from the translation by Dr. Lionel Giles, *The Sayings of Lao-tzŭ*, Wisdom of the East series, London, 1904.

But it is, I imagine, one of those terms which like "the kingdom of heaven" elude the explanations of reason; which mean everything to those who apprehend them from within, and nothing to those who apprehend them from without. Tao is the creative cause of the universe; it contains the quintessence of reality. "It loves and nourishes all things, but does not act as master." "Production without possession, action without self-assertion, development without domination; this is its mysterious operation." I will quote one or two more sayings, and then you will see how apt and pregnant a symbol of the spirit the Dragon became to those familiar with Lao-tzŭ's ideas. For the Dragon was the power manifested in the power of the waters and the clouds, ever-moving, ever-changing, now destroying, now fructifying and preserving. (Pl. 18.)

"There is nothing in the world more soft and weak than water, yet for attacking things that are hard and strong, there is nothing that surpasses it, nothing that can take its place."

"That which has no substance enters where there is no crevice."

"Tao as it exists in the world is like the great rivers and seas which receive the streams from the valleys."

"The reason why rivers and seas are able to be lords over a hundred mountain streams, is that they know how to keep below them."

"What makes a kingdom great is its being like a down-flowing river, — the central point toward which all the smaller streams under Heaven converge."

Always it is the image of water which is in Lao-tzŭ's thought.

"The highest goodness is like water, for water is excellent in benefiting all things and it does not strive. It occupies the lowest place, which men abhor. And therefore it is near akin to Tao."

Lastly, it is said of Tao: "Being great, it passes on; passing on, it becomes remote; having become remote, it returns." And here the words seem actually to evoke a glimpse of the mighty Dragon as the Chinese painters conceived it, rising from the streams and passing into cloud and returning on itself.

What we are now to consider is an art impregnated with the kind of conceptions which those quotations from Lao-tzŭ will have suggested to you — an art specially and peculiarly Chinese, without parallel in the rest of the world, except in Japan.

73

Man is set in a world of beauty diversified with terror. His spirit goes out to explore it. He is ever seeking to come to terms with the world outside himself, to attain some sort of harmony with the living and vast energies which pervade it, or at least some understanding of them. He may return upon himself, persuaded that all the varied beauty of the material world is an illusion, and that only within the mind is secure reality to be sought. That is the instinct of India; and one of the greatest conceptions of Indian art is the image of the Buddha seated in ecstasy, "still as a flame in a windless place," an ecstasy which has consumed the world to thought.

The attitude of Lao-tzŭ seems to have much in common with the Indian attitude, yet it is, I think, more accessible to our ways of thinking. Indian art and poetry are full of delight in the beauties of this world, because in each glory of sound and sight and smell is found a manifestation of the joy of the Infinite Spirit. But with all that sensitiveness to nature there is no passionate study of nature as a whole. There is no development of pure landscape art, as in China, where there is a deep and abiding sense of the companionship of earth and man. The habit of regarding the world of appearances as illusory is too strong.

The Western spirit accepts the reality of the material world; the Western man sees in it something to be used, forces to be harnessed, pleasures to be enjoyed. The art of the West is full of a vivid sense of the glory of the visible world, still more of the beauty of human beings and human activity. But beyond the beauty of shining streams and green meadows and shadowy trees and blue hills lies something from which it recoils: Space, the all-enveloping, infinite, un-explored Space. Even from those regions of earth where we are most conscious of powers and grandeurs outside humanity, the barren wastes, the solitary mountains, it has recoiled. Here is nothing it can use or deal with. The first travel-ler to see Niagara described it as a hideous spectacle.

The attitude of Lao-tzŭ is different from the Indian, different from the Western attitude of mind. But it is more congenial, more accessible to us than is the Indian view. Lao-tzŭ, while accepting the joy of the senses, apprehends the presence of the One among the many; he feels the power of the Spirit which unifies and ener-gizes all things. But he seems to apprehend

75

this creative spirit by intuition, not by processes of thought; and instead of seeking a refuge from cares and troubles in a citadel of changeless calm he seeks to identify himself with that Spirit as it is manifested in the world; to flow with its endless flowing, to "produce without possession, to act without self-assertion, to develop without domination." For the Taoist, "immortality lay in the eternal change." "Chinese historians," says Okakura, "have always spoken of Taoism as the art of living in the world." And this sense of belonging to the great stream of universal life, permeating all things, begets an exhilaration which is visible in all the creative art inspired by the Taoist spirit. It lifts the human soul into an atmosphere where earthly cares are transcended rather than refused. Thus the Dragon, which in Western art and legend is an evil and horrible monster, has with all his formidable force a kind of playfulness; the artists seem to share in its Protean life, exulting in its power and elemental motion; as Shelley, even though weighed down by the sorrows of existence, exulted in the power of the West Wind.

So Space becomes not a terrifying wall and stop to human questioning, but a home of the liberated spirit, where it flows with the flowing of the Eternal Spirit: the universe is one un-bounded whole. This is the inspiration of the landscape art of China. It is also the secret of that use of emptiness in pictorial design which is peculiarly Chinese.

Hollowness, emptiness — these are words, these are ideas, from which our instincts recoil; they are repugnant. But Lao-tzŭ makes friends with the idea of Space, he makes it companion-able; he dwells on the uses of emptiness. "Clay is moulded into a vessel; the utility of the vessel depends on its hollow interior. Doors and win-dows are cut out in order to make a house; the utility of the house depends on the empty spaces. Thus, while the existence of things may be good, it is the non-existent in them which makes them serviceable." At once we find our-selves seeing things from a fresh angle. There is a picture called "Listening to Music" (Pl. 19), attributed, perhaps rightly, to a figure-painter who flourished at the end of the eighth century. It is hard to think of any Western painting in which the empty spaces are made as significant as they are here: one would almost say even more significant than the figures. The intervals seem brimmed with a listening silence. You feel that the artist dwelt on them, so as to draw out their eloquence. It is, so to speak, space spiritualized. Just to illustrate for a moment the contrast between the instincts of the Chinese artists and those of the Indian artists, we might look at a relief from Amaravati (Pl. 20). It is only fair to say that this, like the numerous other reliefs on the Stupa, was an enrichment of a plain surface. But the relief itself, an illustration of the Buddha legend, exemplifies the characteristic Indian love of crowded and clustered forms. I do not mean to disparage this sculpture; for here, as we saw at Ajanta and Bagh, the Indian artist, without any formal symmetry or obvious arrangement, has made a kind of natural harmony of forms abounding with vitality. It makes one think of Blake's exclamation: "Exuberance is Beauty." It is like the beauty of a grape-vine, heavy with its ripe clusters of fruit. The more it is contemplated, the more it reveals an inexhaustible richness of related forms. I merely want to illustrate in a vivid way the extreme contrast of conception in design. And turning back to China, we might instance the beautiful roll in the Boston Museum, a picture of "Ladies preparing Silk," in which again the empty spaces are as beautiful as the forms they enclose (Pl. 21). The actual painting is attributed to the Emperor Hui Tsung, about whom I shall have more to say in a moment; he lived in the eleventh century. But, whoever painted it, it represents, like the "Listening to Music," a design of the preceding era of the T'ang.

But it is time to pass on to Chinese landscape; for it is in landscape that those ideas of which I have been speaking received their complete expression. We pass from the usage of silence and the usage of emptiness, which even in everyday existence, as in the house with its hollow spaces, assists us in the art of living in the world, from the silences which are eloquent as intervals in the painters' figure-design — we pass from these to the outer air, to the all-enclosing space of the universe.

Landscape art in the Chinese estimation is the greatest kind of painting because it includes all forms of life, the abundance of nature and the activities of man.

I said "landscape." But the very word evokes a different conception from the Chinese word, and different associations. It suggests the earth, the countryside, the refreshment from nature that we all crave for, the portraiture of

79

particular places which we delight to visit in memory. The earliest European landscape-paintings, such as the little frescoes from Pompeii, reflecting I suppose the survival of Greek traditions, are conceived as a sort of setting, in the manner of a scene in the theatre, for episodes from Greek legend. Rocks and sea and foliage are not there so much for their own sake as to complete the scene. But the pure landscape art of the West, as we know it, is a late growth, and derives from two main schools, a Southern and a Northern. Titian paints the glory of his own Alpine region of Cadore, the great clouds brooding over valleys of intense pure blue, the nearer verdure overshadowed by gracious trees. Annibale Carracci and Poussin use similar elements in a colder, more formal design: both excel in the broad planning of the masses. Claude brings in the sunlight glittering on calm seas and harbours, foiled by the richness of Southern foliage. In the North, Van Eyck and the brothers Limbourg had already become more intimate with nature than the Southerners in miniatures illustrating manuscripts. The Books of Hours with their pictures of the seasons lead on to the splendid work of Pieter Brueghel. The Dutchmen give us the faithful portraiture of places bathed in atmosphere. Rubens, born composer as he is, adds a vehemence, ease, and breadth, a glory of colour. Elsheimer, Rembrandt, and Seghers impart a deeper and more solemn mode of feeling. Constable builds a noble art out of his deep understanding of the things he loves, showery skies and elms and watered meadows. Turner paints the sea in its grandeur and force as no one else has ever painted it, and the infinite subtleties of light. Whistler evokes the tenderness of twilight and darkness. The French Impressionists attempt the actual vibration of sunshine; then in recoil from the study of atmosphere Cézanne struggles to seize the structure of things in a passion for solidity.

To name these names is to call up many magnificent pictures. The aims and methods of these artists are diverse; but they all have something in common. It is aspects of nature that are painted, the soft or the rugged, the homely or sublime: only rarely, as in the late work of Turner, is there a vision of nature as an infinite whole. It may well be thought that Western landscape has one great superiority over the Chinese landscape; and that is in colour. The Chinese landscapes are painted in ink on silk or

81

paper. Many of the finest are in ink alone. The drawing is always in ink, but the ink foundation may be light-coloured or full-coloured. Nowhere, however, do we find the effects of light, and resultant splendour of colour, such as the Western masters have delighted in. No one could accuse the Chinese of being deficient in a sense for colour; their reticence in this kind of painting must therefore be deliberate. It was an instinctive aversion to dwelling too much on the local colour of things, and their surface appearance. A Chinese critic says: "Colouring in a true pictorial sense does not mean a mere aplication of variegated pigments. The natural aspect of an object can be beautifully conveyed by ink-colour, if one knows how to produce the required shades." [1]

The Chinese word for "landscape" means "mountain-water picture," and suggests at once something more elemental. It is concerned with that which is solid and that which is fluid. The mountains are thought of as the flesh, and the streams as the blood, of a living organism.

It is not the life of nature conceived of as something separate from the life of man, but

[1] Quoted by Sei-ichi Taki, *Three Essays on Oriental Painting*, London, 1910, p. 66.

the whole created universe through which one spirit streams.

Why did the Chinese develop a landscape art so much earlier than Europe? Why is this art almost peculiar to them among the peoples of Asia, except the Japanese who continued their traditions?

It has been suggested that agriculture, being their grand occupation from time immemorial, made it natural for them to be interested in the earth and the seasons. But with other agricultural peoples no such art has arisen.

Again, the making of landscapes, especially the long rolls, has been said to arise from the practice of making maps for military purposes. This practice no doubt contributed much to the development of landscape-painting on the technical side. And if to me it seems that the special virtue and significance as well as the early rise of Chinese landscape derive from mental and spiritual outlook, and mainly from those conceptions of the universe which we have been considering, yet we must not overlook the rational and practical basis of the Chinese character. We find in fact great attention paid to the technical side of the art; and certain phases and schools of landscape-

83

painting are of a homely, almost prosaic character.

To artists unprovided through the accumulated experience of many generations with convenient means of representation, landscape presents material very difficult to cope with. How to relate and unify all these lavish, complex, intricate forms? How to relate the earth and the sky, foreground and distance?

In that early painting ascribed to Ku K'ai-chih of the fourth century, which we considered in my first lecture, the landscape is the only primitive feature. By the eighth century we already find critics ridiculing the landscape of the earlier age, with its "mountains like hair-combs and men as big as mountains."

There is a wall-painting at Tun-huang which is thought to date from about 700 A.D.[1] And though not a landscape, — the subject is a fight for Buddha's relics, — and unfinished, the painting is of great interest, for it shows that the artists have by now come to terms with their material and have evolved the conventions of representation which are at the base of the fully mature art. It is remarkable for the sense of

[1] Reproduced by Waley, *Introduction to Chinese Painting*, London, 1923, Pl. 17.

84

space, reality, openness. The painter's interest does not stop at the limits of the scene he is representing.

I mentioned last week the Buddhist frescoes of Wu Tao-tzŭ, the greatest of all Chinese painters by all repute and the greatest master of the splendid T'ang period. He lived in the eighth century. He also painted landscapes; and a pair of landscapes in Japan are traditionally ascribed to him, but are undoubtedly of later date. Perhaps there is rather more reason in supposing a famous "Waterfall," also in Japan, though this also must be of later date, to echo at least the style of Wu Tao-tzŭ's contemporary Wang Wei, renowned not only as a painter but as a poet. (Pl. 22.)

Wang Wei is said to have originated a school of landscape which aimed at spontaneity of impression, as opposed to the formal style in vogue. He preferred to paint in ink, instead of in greens and blues veined with lines of gold. A celebrated painting of his is known by engravings on stone from which rubbings were taken, and by later copies. One of these, made many centuries later, is in the British Museum. It was a picture of the poet-painter's estate, and was in the form of a long horizontal roll.

85

These rolls, sometimes of immense length, have no counterpart in Western painting. We have friezes, it is true; but these are meant to be seen all at once, whereas the Chinese rolls are meant to be looked at bit by bit, as one reads a book. They have in fact the same form as the manuscripts; and painting in China, as is well known, is considered a branch of handwriting.

The other form of painting was the hanging picture, which was appropriate to such subjects as the "Waterfall" of Wang Wei, where the painter has chosen a single motive abstracted from nature, presenting no complex problems of structure and perspective. It is the force and weight of falling water that has impressed him; and what fitter subject for the ink-charged Chinese brush?

We must pass now to the age of Sung, the dynasty which lasted from 960 to 1260 A.D., a space of three hundred years, divided into two periods, Northern Sung and Southern Sung; for early in the twelfth century the Golden Tartars invaded and conquered Northern China.

In the year 1100 there came to the throne a young prince, Hui Tsung, who was devoted to aesthetic pursuits and himself a painter. In the preceding T'ang period another emperor, Ming

Huang, had surrounded himself with poets, painters, and musicians. The Chinese were always inclined to see things from the aesthetic point of view, but he carried the worship of beauty to an extreme never known in the West. Hui Tsung sought to rival Ming Huang. He founded an Academy of Calligraphy and Painting, and made a vast collection. But like his predecessor, he came to an unhappy end. He was captured by the Tartars and died in captivity.

There is little left of the painting of Northern Sung. It was marked by a certain deliberate naturalism. The artists of the Academy were exhorted to draw from the life, rather than copy old masters, but nobility of line was also insisted on.

In Japan are a pair of pictures of lotuses, assigned by tradition to a famous master of the tenth century (Pl. 23). Here is fidelity to nature, but still more are we struck by the nobility of line; a grandeur united to delicacy and an attitude to the life of flowers such as would astonish us in any European painter. For the flowers are not regarded as delightful accessories to human life but are contemplated as living things, of a dignity not less than that of human beings. The force of flowers springing up

87

through the soil and, erect upon slender stems, poising in the air and trembling; their sensitiveness, their slow or swift expansion from secret bud to splendid blossom — it is these rather than their lovely colour and texture that were the motives for this art.

The same artist is said to have painted a beautiful picture, also preserved in Japan, of a white heron on a snowy bough. Again, there is exquisite observation, yet it is not merely observation from outside. We feel something more: the artist has identified himself with the object of his contemplation. The bird is seen in isolation, yet if isolated to the eye it is not isolated to the mind; it is subtly related both to ourselves and to the world about it. It is the miracle of art that what is in a man's mind, not only his conscious aim but the imponderable stirrings and promptings that colour his conception of life, passes into what he makes.

We might well divine in such paintings a tinge of religious feeling. And in fact when we come to the art of Southern Sung, this religious tinge is more definitely revealed. It came from the Zen sect of Buddhism, which in this period had a peculiar influence on both thought and art.

When the Northern part of the Empire fell

into the hands of the Tartars the capital was removed to the South, to Hang-chow. This is the wonderful city described by Marco Polo, after it too had fallen under the Tartar domination in the thirteenth century. It was a far more civilized place than any contemporary city in Europe. The inhabitants neither wore arms nor kept them in their houses; they were especially courteous and welcoming to foreigners. The neighbourhood of Hang-chow, with its lakes and mountains, is of peculiar beauty. The sense of defeat and wounded pride in the loss of the Northern provinces rankled with many; others found abundant solace in the life of contemplation.

Such circumstances may well have proved propitious to the growth of Zen Buddhism, which had been in existence for several centuries but now became a power in art. According to Zen doctrine it was a vain thing to seek for Buddha through religious ceremonies and observances; even prayer, even the reading of the sacred scriptures, was of no value. Why? Because Buddha is Thought, beyond speech or writing. The deepest truth cannot be spoken or written down. Each must seek for Buddha, the Absolute, in his own heart.

So now, rather than the great Bodhisattvas, rather than the Western Paradise, it was the Arhats, the immediate disciples of Buddha, seated in a fixity of intense thought, who became the favourite themes of Buddhist painting.

A certain affinity with Taoist doctrine is obvious in Zen. "The Tao which can be expressed in words is not the eternal Tao"; and in fact there seems to be in this period a sort of coalescence of Taoism with Zen Buddhism. The Arhats have their Taoist counterparts in the Rishi, the mountain-dwellers who have become so dematerialized that they can float in the air at will and live on mountain dew; just as Bodhidharma, the founder of the Zen sect, is often represented crossing the ocean on a reed.

Whether Zen or Taoism was the more potent influence on Sung landscape, who shall say? I should imagine that this art really owed most to Taoism, or let us say that side of the Chinese genius which Lao-tzŭ and his followers expressed. In any case there is the art itself; and at last we can point to something more than hints and fragments. The Japanese, when they reconstructed two centuries later the Sung culture, collected with enthusiasm the landscapes of Southern Sung; hence these are richly represented in Japan. But the Boston Museum alone has enough — more indeed, than all Europe can boast — to illustrate the essential character of this art.

Already in the eleventh century, the earlier part of this period, a famous painter, Kuo Hsi, had written an essay on landscape. What are the things he insists on? First he explains the love of landscape as something innate in man: to get away from the dust and noise of the world to the companionship of woods and springs, mists and vapours, is to realize one's true self. The finest landscapes are those in which one can wander, in which one can live. He has much to say about the painting of mountains, "the divinely beautiful mountains," about trees, and mists and water. Each must have its own life; water must flow and murmur, clouds move, mountains have their light and shade. To render this, there must be a corresponding life in the brush; and for this there needs the utmost concentration of mind. The essential features must be seized; no mere skill can achieve this. It is the mental effort that is insisted on, the intellectual, the imaginative grasp.

It is rather hard for us, used to the practice of painting from nature with the eye on the object, to realize what intensity of contemplation preceded the actual throwing of the preconceived design with swift immediate strokes on the absorbent silk or paper. No elaboration by the busy hand, while the mind remains idle! All must be seen in memory or imagined; then the full mind's conception overbrims into form and tone.

Such a method could hardly have been possible without the long training of the hand necessary for the writing of Chinese characters. And not of hand only: for what is valued in handwriting is not different from what is valued in painting: the virtual identity of the two arts is often stressed. We in the West have the nobility of the Roman lettering. A fine Roman or Italian inscription is a thing that thrills with the beauty of what is enduring and august. We can show some superb examples of handwriting, but these are not common, nor do we cultivate writing as an art. The Chinese union of writing and painting is best seen in the ink paintings of that favourite motive, the bamboo. In such painting the brush strokes would have an immediacy of communication, whereby the inmost nature of the artist was revealed, over and above his skill. But probably no Westerner can ever appreciate to the full the subtleties of difference in quality and expressiveness.

When we read the descriptions of handwriting by famous masters it is manifest that something much more than mere skill was valued; just as the bamboo was chosen not only because the form of its stem and leaves lent itself so well to brush-drawing, but because it symbolized the kind of character most admired by the Chinese, the character which yields and bends before the storms of life but does not break: it is graceful but also strong. The handwriting of one of the most famous calligraphers, Mi Fei, was compared by one admirer to the play of a sharp sword in the hands of a master of fence, and by another to the movements of a mettlesome horse under a rider who controls him without aid of bit or bridle.[1]

Mi Fei painted landscapes. There are many attributed to him, though it is doubtful if any original exists; but he was above all renowned as a writer and as a collector. Once in a boat with some friends he was shown a masterpiece of handwriting and threatened at once to jump overboard if it was not given to him. He obtained his desire; he amassed a precious collec-

[1] See Sirén, *Early Chinese Painting*, London, 1933, vol. II, p. 28.

tion; but he was extremely particular as to those to whom he showed his treasures. No hand but his own was to touch a painting that he possessed.

Mi Fei, who lived in the eleventh century, was one of a group of distinguished scholars famous for their power with brush and ink, whether in writing or painting. His style in landscape was expressive of poetic mood and exalted feeling, his favourite motive conical peaks rising from the woods; but it lent itself easily to mannered imitation. And when imitated without the intensity of mood which the master pours into his brush, this kind of landscape soon wears thin.

It is when we come to the painters of Southern Sung, a little later, that the art of landscape comes to full fruition. Its special distinction is that while it has a solid basis of observation, and a strong grasp of all the variety of natural form, it is suffused with poetic feeling. These landscapes were mostly the work of professional artists. Much of Chinese landscape is the work of poets and calligraphers who painted only when they were in the mood; and their painting, especially in later times, becomes airy and unsubstantial, charming when one surrenders to

94

its peculiar mood, but overmuch detached from reality.

In the chief masters of Southern Sung, there is a virile mastery of the structure of things. In some the line is predominant, in others it is tone. Though you may miss the sensuous appeal of colour, it is after all the relations of tone in colouring which give unity and vitality to a picture. What is amazing is the way in which these painters, working in ink and water-colour, succeed in expressing the conformation of the earth as well as the effects of atmosphere and of distance, with a persuasion of reality not less than Western artists achieve in the more solid medium of oils. They had inherited a gradually matured technical tradition which trained them in the various means of representation, they had an assured foundation of craftsmanship; and this set them free to put their whole force into the emotion they wished to communicate. It is by the quality of that emotion no less than by their intellectual grasp that we judge of their achievement.

This landscape art of Sung has been called Romantic, and also Idealistic. I sometimes wish that terms like these had never been invented. They are useful to critics, but they often serve

as labels which we attach to artists or their
works in order to dispense with the trouble of
further thinking. Let us attempt a little more
precision. These landscapes have been called
Romantic, I suppose, because they are conceived of as an escape from the realities of life.
Indeed their character has been explained by the
fact that China had suffered a great defeat; and
though similar landscapes had been painted
before the Northern provinces were conquered,
the circumstances may have had some influence
on the art. We in the West call art and poetry
Romantic when they deal with the strange and
remote, when they represent a rebellion from
the routine of existence, a craving for the wild,
the marvellous, even the abnormal. The Chinese
poets and artists also rebel against the routine
of existence, since they were so often compelled
to take up official posts; but if they crave for the
companionship of hills and streams, it is because they are convinced that in such companionship the true life of man is to be found. It is
an escape not from life, but to life. Therefore
these paintings are mostly serene and exhilarating. Nor is there anything unreal about them;
it is no dream-world that they create. European
Romantics, like Salvator Rosa, cultivated a

fashionable wildness, painting horrid crags, with
brigands round the corner; and these pictures
are steeped in unreality; that was their attrac-
tion. In the Sung landscapes there is no such
make-believe. To these artists the term "inanimate nature" would have seemed incompre-
hensible. The painter was told that in painting rocks rising from a river he must make
one feel that the rock beneath the water is
there, as real as the portion that is visible.
That is just an instance of the way in which
the landscape-painter's art was conceived. He
must identify himself with what he paints, become what he contemplates, before he can
express it truly. This may not be what is
called realism; it is something better, it is to
deal with reality.

I recall a little painting, of uncertain date but
inspired by a poem of Wang Wei's, the eighth-
century poet-painter; the subject is just a sparse
wood of stunted trees on a flat foreland; misty
water and still sky. Nothing of grandeur, nothing of the picturesque; nothing of what to the
average mind is beautiful; yet in this forlorn
scene there was something strangely moving,
just because the painter had absorbed that solitude of trees and water into himself. He had

painted it internally, so to speak, not as something alien and seen from the outside.

Nor do these artists shrink from the vastness of empty space. They discover in it their own liberation.

Mr. Berenson has pointed out the peculiar value given to space in compositions of the Umbrian school in Italy. They are designed in depth, and the eye is led onward to a luminous vacancy, emphasized it may be, and given an added value, by architectural forms, such as the framing of an arch, the central feature of the composition. There are pictures by Perugino and Raphael in which this use of space reveals an extraordinary beauty. In what do they differ from those of the Chinese masters? There is a difference: and I think it is this. With the Umbrians the key-note is peace; a consummation of repose beyond the activities of mankind. It is an ennobling serenity, giving largeness and ease to attitude and gesture. But with the Chinese, space often becomes the protagonist in the design. It is not a final peace, but itself an activity flowing out from the picture into our minds, and drawing us up into a rarer atmosphere. It is tranquillizing, but even more it is exhilarating.

The two greatest masters of the period are

Hsia Kuei and Ma Yüan. I wish I could show you a long roll by Hsia Kuei which is in Peking. It is called "The River of Ten Thousand Li" and is over thirty feet long. As it is unrolled, we pass down the great stream, now flowing full and smooth, now fretted into rapids and swirling in eddies; it foams past rocks, it glides under willows; and we have the feeling that we cannot help having about noble rivers, that they have a sort of living personality of their own. An admirable theme for this peculiarly Chinese form of painting, the long horizontal scroll. But to show only a section is to do such a painting an injustice. The small picture by the master reproduced on Plate 25 is typical of his style.

By Ma Yüan, again, there is a great scroll-painting in the Freer Gallery at Washington. It is now catalogued as a copy; but copy or not, there is no more grandly designed landscape in the world. At the first opening of the roll we are taken straight into the heart of the mountains; we breathe keen mountain air. It is a picture in which one can wander all day long. Descending the hills, one sees the gleam of a lake receding into sunny mist. Here and there are fishermen's cottages; higher up are pavilions among woods. All becomes soft and tranquil, and then suddenly tower before us perpendicular cliffs, a huge table of rock, down which a water-fall plunges into foam. Open space again; water and reed-beds and a flight of wild geese in the air; the hills grow distant; all is homelier; serene horizons expand beyond; and then again, with a final note of majesty and aloofness, tall pinnacles of rock crowd together and soar abruptly. The themes melt into each other, or are vigorously contrasted; the whole makes up a tremendous full-toned harmony. You can infer something of the character of that scroll-painting, or at least some aspects of it, from smaller pictures by the master, in which rock-pinnacles of the Yang-tse tower in the mist above the water, where perhaps a fisherman's boat will be moored below crags and storm-beaten pines. Such are the elements out of which a thousand landscapes will be composed by later generations of artists: and we may well become tired of the eternal twisted pines and peaks and mists and water. But when we come back to the great masters, such as Ma Yüan, all is fresh again; we feel what he has felt. As I said in my first lecture, we can always tell how finely or how coarsely organized is the nature

which confronts us in any creation of art. Are
we conscious of any intervening veil of time
between ourselves and such pictures as these?
Can we not enter without any feeling of strange-
ness into the mind behind the little picture in
the Boston Museum reproduced on Plate 26?
Is it not a remarkable thing that not only seven
hundred years in time and half the width of the
globe in space but a total difference of race, of
training, of modes of thought, should fail to
separate our minds from the mind that made
these pictures? It is the beginning of spring
among the mountains, the willows have begun
to put forth their green tassels; rain has fallen,
the sky is clear. The painter's brush tracing
the boughs of the willow is so sensitive that he
almost persuades us that the boughs and young
leaves are sentient things themselves, and as
Wordsworth says "enjoy the air they breathe."
It is such a morning perhaps as the English poet
commemorated in those lines beginning

It is the first mild day of March

and ending

Have I not reason to lament
What man has made of man?

Another treasure of the Boston Museum is
also ascribed to Ma Yüan (Pl. 27). Many of the

Sung landscapes are without any figures; many show a sage in the foreground contemplating a waterfall or the moon, or a solitary fisherman in his boat. These are "landscapes with figures," as we say, rather than "figures in a landscape." Here the figure of the woman, who was a Buddhist mystic of the T'ang period, fills the eye, though the landscape is no mere background, but seems almost as if it were a projection from her mind, as she wanders out on the wintry shore beyond the snow-covered trees. What are her thoughts? We cannot tell. But at least, without any external knowledge, we are sure that she is not hurrying to an appointment, nor occupied with household cares, nor is she just thinking how cold it is. In some subtle way we are made to feel that she is tasting solitude with a kind of ecstasy. Is it because the solitude, the frozen earth and the empty air, enable her to feel more poignantly the unreality of all but thought? Is it because in that stillness she can melt her spirit into the infinite surrounding her? In all times and in all lands the mystic is the same: his longing is the flight of "the Alone to the Alone."

Here certainly we meet the spirit of Zen, which, as I said, coloured the Taoist concep-

tions implicit in so much of the Sung painting
with a special tinge. We shall find the Zen
mode of thought a still more potent, and even
the dominant, factor in the art of fifteenth-
century Japan. In China, I think, it is visible
chiefly in the preference for motives which suggest rather than display. For though the loftiest
reach of the Sung masters is to be seen in their
paintings of great heights and spaces, in which
the mind could bathe, each painting of flower
or reed or bird was informed by the same spirit.
It was like a note of music implying all the related harmonies of existence. A spray of blossom trembling in the wind seemed to be at once
an apparition from a world of intenser life and
a kind of secret thought unfolding in the heart
of man. I recall one small painting of hibiscus
in which only half of the blossom is visible,
hovering over its reflection in the water; nothing is wholly shown, everything is suggested.

In showing these few examples of Sung landscape, you may think I have talked too much
about the world of ideas in which they were
born; you may think that perhaps I have read
my own fancies into them. Ignore, then, all
that; regard them as they are, and for what
they give you. Is it not manifest that it is no

merely visual impression, no merely physical sensation that they communicate? It is something more. It may be that the conscious part of the artist was absorbed in his design, in achieving a right relation of tone to tone, in tracing lines that should be alive. But whether consciously or no, he was doing more than this, because what he put into his work comes out from it and flows over into our minds; and we recognize something which cannot be called intellectual only, or sensuous only, or emotional only; it is a wholeness of spirit which goes out, free and unafraid, into the wholeness of the universe. The finest landscapes, to quote Kuo Hsi again, are those one can wander in, those one can live in.

Here, remote from us in time, remote from us in space, deriving nothing from the culture and science which have been our Western heritage, is an art that is near to us as anything contemporary with ourselves.

PLATE 17

BRONZE NATARAJA. SOUTH INDIA

PLATE 18

NINE DRAGONS (DETAIL), BY CH'EN JUNG. CHINA, *ca.* 1235-1255 A.D.

PLATE 19

LISTENING TO MUSIC (DETAIL), ATTRIBUTED TO CHOU FANG. CHINA, *ca.* 780–810 A.D.

PLATE 20

BUDDHIST SCENE. STONE RELIEF FROM THE GREAT
STUPA AT AMARAVATI. INDIA, 2ND–3RD CENTURY A.D.

PLATE 21

LADIES PREPARING SILK (DETAIL), BY HUI TSUNG. CHINA, 1082–1135 A.D.

PLATE 22

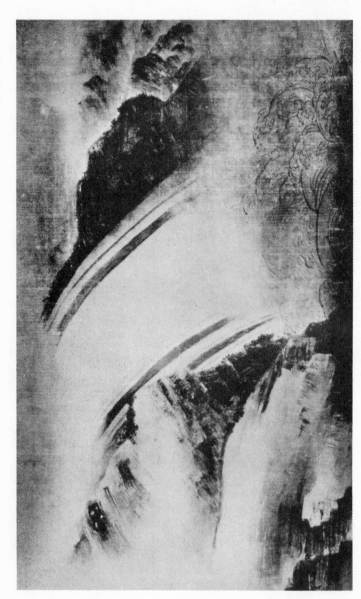

WATERFALL, ATTRIBUTED TO WANG WEI. CHINA, 698-759 A.D.

PLATE 23

LOTUSES, ATTRIBUTED TO HSÜ HSI. CHINA,
10TH CENTURY

PLATE 24

LANDSCAPE (DETAIL), BY TUNG YÜAN. CHINA, 10TH CENTURY

PLATE 25

LANDSCAPE, BY HSIA KUEI. CHINA, *ca.* 1180–1230 A.D.

PLATE 26

SPRING LANDSCAPE, BY MA YÜAN. CHINA, 1190–1224 A.D.

PLATE 27

LADY MYSTIC IN THE SNOW, BY MA YÜAN. CHINA, 1190–1224 A.D.

Lecture IV

ART IN PERSIA

WE HAVE seen how the art and thought of India penetrated and inwardly enriched the art of China at the time of its greatest creative vigour under the T'ang dynasty. This was made possible by the fact that India and the Far East were connected by ways of communication, both overland, through the Central Asian trade-route, and by sea.

The Near East, on the other hand, has its natural contacts with the Mediterranean; it faces Westward. Intermediary in its position is the great tableland of Persia; and Persia by its geographical situation was able both to give and to receive, through intercourse with Greece and Byzantium on the one side and with China and India on the other.

In very early periods Persian art, as we see it in the bronzes of animals recently discovered in Luristan, propagated its motives of design among the outlying, unsettled, still nomad tribes who formed the Scythian world and occupied Southern Russia and a great part of Turkestan; and this style spread further into

Siberia, to stimulate and enrich the art of the Han dynasty in China.

In historic times the great achievement of Iran was the establishment of a vast empire under the dynasty of the Achaemenids, familiar to us through their attempted conquest of Greece, and their final overthrow by Alexander.

To the Greek world, Asia meant the Persian Empire. Those of us who have been brought up on the classics, who have been thrilled in our schooldays by the story of Marathon and Thermopylae, may find it hard to get rid of the prejudices clinging to those old associations. It is natural for us to take the Greek side in the contest between Europe and Asia, and to have our thoughts tinged with the Greek feeling of apprehension lest European civilization should be swamped by barbarian Asia, mingled with a certain contempt for Asiatic luxury.

Yet Persia under the Achaemenid dynasty was itself a great civilization. It was "the first really organized empire of the ancient world," famous for its great roads and its magnificent palaces. It owed something to Assyria and something to Egypt, but had its own character. A single small work in bronze and gold, the winged ibex now in Berlin, may give us a clue

to the Persian style of this period. Marvellous
as the Assyrian reliefs of animals in hunting
scenes are, they lack something which we find
here: an elegance combined with vigour, a
sensitiveness, a nervous force, a purity of form
— qualities which we shall find later in Persia's
mature art. (Pl. 28.)

From about 550 to 330 B.C. this great empire
flourished. Then it fell before the genius, the
will and power, of Alexander.

I quoted in my second lecture the contemptu-
ous response of the Indian ascetics to Alexander's questions and invitations. It is interesting
to compare their attitude with the Persian one.
To those Indians all action was not only un-
necessary and undesirable, but unreal; they
saw no meaning whatever in Alexander's vic-
tories. The Persian, on the contrary (if we may
take the poet Nizami for representative), accepted the conquest of the world as a momentous event, not so much in itself as for what it
made possible. For we are told that after con-
quering the world Alexander gathered together
the intellectual and spiritual fruits of his vic-
tories: all the chief books of the conquered
countries were translated, and new rules of conduct were promulgated. Sages come from afar

to the conqueror's court; they ask him such questions as "Where is the invisible God to be sought for?" and Alexander answers them. And now, having attained the rank of a prophet, he starts on a second expedition over the world; he marches West to Andalusia and the African Desert and the ultimate Ocean, and south to India, and east to China, and finally in the North he finds a people whose manners are still of the Golden Age, and decides that after all the life of solitude and contemplation is the best.

To the Persian poet so surpassing a spirit as Alexander could not be conceived of as a mere stormer of cities; he must be a warrior commissioned by heaven to make war on the crimes, the follies, the ignorance of mankind.

That is a romantic conception, if you will; but you cannot call it barbarian. The Persians are a romantic race — there is no denying it — incurably romantic. They enjoy the improbable and incredible. They like the heroes of stories to be fabulously brave, and the heroines dazzlingly beautiful. This, from a modern point of view, is no doubt a severe limitation to their art. Yet it is from its very limitations that Persian painting wins its unique charm.

A Persian painter of the fifteenth century con-

ceived Alexander and his privy council of Seven
Sages, the Seven Wise Men of Greece, as a
group in Persian dress sitting in a garden. That
the great conqueror actually had Aristotle for
his tutor is to the Oriental mind sufficient
ground for including Socrates and Plato, Apol-
lonius of Tyana, the inventor of talismans, and
Hermes Trismegistus, great adept in the secrets
of nature, among the company. Why pedanti-
cally insist on the niceties of chronology? If
these were not all contemporaries, they ought
to have been; if they were not associates of Alexander, then history is to blame. In both East
and West Alexander's glory has been a magnet
to every kind of legend: for centuries, even in
the West, the Romance ousted the facts. But
gradually the Western mind, intent on plain
truth, has cleared away the mists of legend;
Alexander and his exploits stand out in the clear
light of day. Even now scholars are busy in
determining the exact details of his campaigns,
and Sir Aurel Stein has recently discovered the
place at which he crossed the Indus. But as to
these things, dates and localities and other irrelevant particulars, the Persian mind is indif-
ferent.

After all, it is not the military achievements of

Alexander that are significant for later times; it is rather the momentous effects of his great expedition, and the results of his policy toward the peoples conquered, — the uniting of East and West, the attempt to found a world-empire. The Greek language was spread abroad into far lands it would otherwise never have reached. But Alexander did not merely aim to impose Greek civilization on Asia; he put Persians in high places of trust and authority, he readily adopted Persian dress and manners on occasion.

We see how the intellectual glory of Greece has impressed the Persian mind. But Greek art, though through Alexander's conquest it brought new motives of decoration into Iran, had no dominant or enduring influence there.

After Alexander's successors came a Parthian dynasty, which, while it derived much from Hellenistic culture on the West, at the same time carried Iranian influence eastward into India. Parthian kingdoms were established on the lower Indus. Some of these Parthians became Buddhists, and even went as Buddhist missionaries to China.

But much more memorable is the Sasanian dynasty, which ruled Persia from the third century to the seventh century of our era. These kings were themselves Persian, and they consciously revived the glories of the Achaemenid line both in politics and in the arts.

The Sasanian dynasty was the last line of kings of native blood which was to rule over Persia till the rise of the Safavi dynasty in the sixteenth century. For nine centuries the country was under alien rulers. No wonder that the Persians looked back with a special fondness to the great Sasanian dynasty, and loved to celebrate the deeds of the heroes of that time in poetry and art.

The history of Persia is truly singular. Conquest after conquest sweeps over the land, some bringing unheard-of havoc and bloodshed; yet a persistent vitality renews itself and refuses to succumb. And as with the nation, so with its art. One might expect to find the native style quite obliterated by the influx of foreign ideas and foreign forms; but no, it emerges, timidly at first, but slowly and surely establishes itself afresh.

The most remarkable of these conquests was the Arab conquest in the seventh century, which swept away the last Sasanian king; remarkable, because it was the triumph not only of invading arms but of an aggressive religion.

We have seen how great a part Buddhism played in the development of Indian art, as later in the art of China; and we shall see how fruitful an inspiration it became in the art of Japan. But here we are confronted with a religion which, so far from encouraging the painter and the sculptor to portray the forms of sacred and celestial beings, or illustrate sacred legend, regards such a practice as impious and shrinks from it in horror. This attitude to representative art was taken over by Muhammad from Judaism.

You may remember the scornful words of the author of "The Wisdom of Solomon" when he describes how a carpenter, having made from a tree a vessel fit for the service of man's life, takes the very refuse, a crooked piece of wood and full of knots, and carves it "when he had nothing else to do" into the image of a man, or like some vile beast, laying it over with vermilion. How aptly though how unsympathetically he describes the born artist, eyeing a piece of wood and seeing in it the form that he wants to liberate from it, irresistibly attracted by its potentiality and carving it in the leisure left him from his task-work! But the very fact that the writer is so scornful and angry over the artist and his

carving betrays the force of the instinct he in-
veighs against. These images have no life, he
protests; but they *have* life. The magic of art
is that it *can* create "forms more real than living
man." We do not look on these images as we do
on facts; they are in a different world. If in a
picture, or statue, or poem, a fact remains a
fact, something outside ourselves, there is no art.

We can understand, then, the fear of idolatry;
but it is a little difficult to realize the state of
mind of those who thought that to paint living
forms in a picture was a sin more heinous than
murder, and that to sit for one's portrait was to
connive at a practice of scandalous depravity.
The explanation doubtless is that the Arabs had
no instinct and no gift for pictorial or plastic art.
In the Persians on the contrary the instinct and
gift were so deeply implanted that no outside
influence could suppress them.

The Arabs brought from their burning des-
erts a pure and lofty monotheism, a surpassing
enthusiasm for the faith, and a will to conquer.
The impetus, the swiftness and completeness,
of the movement with which Islam swept over
so many countries is one of the wonders of
history.

Of all the races of the Nearer East, who were

now united under the Islamic theocracy, the
Persians were the most gifted in art and architecture. As architects they produced masterpieces. In pottery their design and workmanship
have never been surpassed. But I will confine
myself to painting, because there we can trace
the growth of a national style from its early
budding to its ripe perfection. Unfortunately,
the destruction has been so immense that the
actual material surviving is, for the early centuries, sadly meagre.

If we ask what tradition it was that the Arab
conquest interrupted, we can point to very little
which can serve as a document. Actually the
earliest Iranian paintings known are, strange to
say, Buddhist. These are frescoes recently
found by M. Hackin in Afghanistan; and Sasanian princes and courtiers are there depicted
with Buddhist monks. They date from the fifth
century. At Tak-i-Bustan there are sculptured
reliefs of hunting scenes which recall later
Persian painting, while also reminding us of
Assyrian reliefs in stone.

But there was also in Sasanian times a special
tradition of religious painting.

In the year 1904 a German expedition, working under Von Le Coq in the desert sites of Cen-

tral Asia, discovered near Turfan a Manichaean temple. The temple contained large wall-paintings and fragments of illuminated manuscripts. Before this time Manichaeism had been considered merely as a Christian heresy. It was founded by Mani, a Persian, in the third century after Christ. That period was a time of great religious ferment; and Mani, we now know, conceived the idea of making a new world-religion out of elements derived from Zoroastrianism, Christianity, and Buddhism. His religion gave great encouragement to art; and, more than this, Mani was himself a painter. In Persian literature his name is referred to as the typical painter of old; if an artist was praised, he was said to paint like Mani. His renown was all the more secure in that none of his works were known. He himself was less fortunate; he was put to death by order of Bahram, King of Persia, about the year 274. His religion made remarkable progress in the East and on both shores of the Mediterranean, but was severely persecuted, and the last of those persecutions drove the Manichaeans into Central Asia: so that the fragments in those regions, now at Berlin, are all that survives of what must once have been a very active school of religious art.

The rather haphazard growth and mixed character of the early painting may be partly set down to a condition that was to remain. We have to do with an art created less by local schools, with their roots in a certain soil, than by artists working now at this court, now at that, according as they found patrons to support them. Though princes and potentates ignored the orthodox prohibition, and painting began to flourish, still the theologians continued inflexibly to frown on the art; there was no patronage from the Church. Instead of this, the artists had to work for individual patrons and to please their taste. There was no public art. And however much prized by their own patrons, the painters and their art were in general held in no great honour.

One thing must be noted, however. While the painter was little esteemed, the calligrapher had high repute. His art was accounted altogether superior to that of the painter; for what more laudable act than to copy in exquisite script the Word of God?

We may take it for certain that there was a pictorial art in Persia before the Arab invasion, and in the East and North-east Manichaean and Buddhist traditions probably survived. But

the centre of Islamic power, the seat of the
Caliphs, was in Mesopotamia, in Baghdad; and
though the culture prevailing there was Persian,
the style of painting practised in Mesopotamia
was founded rather on Mediterranean art.
Doubtless for a longish period the prohibition
of painting prevailed; but gradually, as the Arab
rulers assimilated Persian culture, they paid less
attention to it and grew easier in their attitude
to painting. The Mesopotamian painting, as
we know it, consists of illustrations to Arabic
manuscripts. There is at first but little trace of
a definitely Persian element; the style seems to
derive mainly from late classical art, especially
from Christian paintings and mosaics. In its
main character it is Western rather than Eastern. There is free and lively drawing of the
human figure, but little interest in anything else.

The most important relic of the painting produced at Baghdad is a famous manuscript of
the Arab author Hariri in the Bibliothèque
Nationale. This is exceptionally animated. The
manuscript is full of vivid scenes of contemporary life, the life of the thirteenth century.
We feel that though it may spring from a decaying tradition, it is the work of an artist who
has zest and vigour, who has his eye on the ob-

117

ject. In most of the surviving productions of
this school, while the figure-design has a certain largeness of style as well as animation, the
forms of vegetation seem drawn by people who
had never looked at flowers or trees, who took
no delight in seeing how plants grow. The
patterns on the dresses also appear to be copied
without understanding from earlier work; there
is nothing of the true decorator's instinct for
seizing and adapting motives from nature.

What will become of this art? It seems to be
developing in the atmosphere of the Mediterranean mind, with a Western, not an Eastern,
tendency. But soon a different element makes
itself felt.

Look at an illustration to the Fables of Bidpay — a monkey throwing figs to a turtle — and
then at another illustration to the same fable
(Pl. 29). The trees are growing, the wind is in
their leaves. We are in contact here with something very different from the decaying formulas
of Hellenism; we feel a breath from the mature
and masterly art of China.

During the period of the Caliphate, in the
eastern parts of Persia, trade with China was
extensive. In the first half of the thirteenth century Asia was overrun by the terrible armies of

Jinghis Khan. The Mongols were already masters of China when they conquered Persia, and they brought Chinese artists with them. And in the fourteenth century we find manuscripts in which the painters are plainly trying to assimilate the Chinese style. Two manuscripts which have survived are specially remarkable; one is the "History of the World," a manuscript which is divided between Edinburgh University and the Royal Asiatic Society in London. As illustrations, these are of fascinating interest. As art, also: for here we see an attempt to imitate Chinese style by artists who have been trained in a different tradition. They limit their colour and draw in ink like the Chinese; they paint landscape, of which the Chinese were masters; but in the treatment both of water and of mountains they tend to freeze the bold Chinese conventions into mere decoration. What was fluid becomes stagnant. They are obviously not interested in the world of nature.

The other manuscript is a Shah-namah, the Book of the Kings, the enormous epic completed by Firdausi early in the eleventh century. This manuscript was broken up on its arrival in Europe (Pls. 30 and 31). Many of the fifty-four paintings which it contained are in American museums and collections.

Here we have a much more successful effort to assimilate Chinese style. It is as if the painter had seen fine Chinese paintings, had studied them and been keenly stimulated, and had then turned away and worked in his own manner, with that added consciousness behind him. There is no surface imitation of Chinese convention, but there is a new sense of rhythm and vigorous movement, such as we enjoy in the Chinese painting of the fourteenth century.

This manuscript forms a landmark in Persian painting. Splendid in their simple scheme of deep-toned colour, massive force, and dramatic design, these paintings have a masculine style well suited to the epic they illustrate.

This is not yet the fully-formed Persian style; there is still a long process of refinement to be undergone; but it is a phase of great importance for what it contributes to the growing tradition. The Chinese influence has stimulated, has fructified; it passes, and the Persian style begins, as if unconsciously and like a flower springing from long-buried seed, to take root and unfold in a character distinct from all the elements it has absorbed.

Persia, which in the thirteenth century had suffered the devastating invasion of the Mongols, was to endure yet another and even more crushing calamity at the end of the succeeding century. Timur swept over Asia with his triumphant armies; it was like a hunt on a monstrous, a fabulous scale, with no more mercy for men and women than for animals. Destruction for its own sake seemed the aim of this scourge of mankind. City after city was obliterated from the face of the earth.

Yet the bloodthirsty Timur was not only a man of extraordinary powers but a great lover of art. It was his custom to spare the artists in the cities he destroyed and collect them in his capital of Samarcand to work under his own supervision.

Two pages from a manuscript of 1396, one of the very few surviving from the time of Timur, may illustrate how the framework of pictorial conventions was being built up. One depicts a duel in the clearing of a wood between two warriors (Pl. 32). The spectator is assumed to be looking down on the scene from a certain elevation, and this has the effect of making the horizon appear high. We see the difference between the Eastern and the Western approach to the problem of perspective. In Western art, at least since the Renaissance, the effort has been to realize a scene as it would appear in nature. Figures and objects in nature appear smaller in the distance; therefore they must be represented smaller. Parallel lines appear to converge; therefore they must do so in a painting. The question asked is: Does the picture correspond to our visual impressions? And the whole problem has been worked out on a scientific basis. The Persian artist, on the contrary, would say that an appeal to nature is irrelevant. He is making a work of art; and art is called art just because it is not nature. What he is concerned with is to present a scene and tell a story, as eloquently and enjoyably as he can. It may be that persons in the distance are as interesting as those in the foreground. Why then make them unrecognizable? Flowers at a distance become mere smudges to the eye; but that is no reason why we should represent them as smudges. Let them be painted larger, so that we may enjoy their colour, form, and growth. Again, in a night scene we see only shadows; but who can be interested in shadows? The spectator wants to know what is happening. Here is a night scene (Pl. 33), as we see from the

122

moon in the sky; but everything is as clear as day.

This refusal to paint darkness, as also to represent the cast shadow, is characteristic of all Asian painting, except where European methods have influenced the artist. You may think the Persian attitude rather childish; it is indeed still wedded to the methods employed instinctively by children. But at any rate it is not infected by the Western heresy that fidelity to natural effects is a fundamental principle of art.

We come to the fifteenth century. It is the great age of Persian painting. An adorable little picture in the Musée des Arts Décoratifs in Paris dates from the early part of the century (Pl. 34). The Prince Humay, newly arrived at the court of China, is being received in a garden by the Chinese princess, Humayun. The whole scene is redolent of coloured blossom and fragrance. Forms are growing less stiff, plants are becoming less conventional.

This is supposed to be a Chinese scene. But how different it is from a Chinese painting! It is true that there are certain basic conventions in common between the two styles. But it is a different mind that is expressed in a different conception of design. Chinese art knows, as no other art has known, the eloquence of reserves and silences. It uses the power of empty space. The Chinese painters select from nature, but draw natural forms with exquisite observation.

The Persians have a passion for gardens; but the gardens they love are formal ones, full of straight lines and symmetry, such as is abhorrent to Chinese taste. The Chinese like the unsymmetrical, and make balance, not symmetry, their principle. Persian design, then, is more formal; its elements are more solid and static. Chinese painting is full of movement, of breathing wind or floating mist. Persian painting is still, bright, vivid, and unblurred. Again, the Chinese love sober and low-toned colour; the Persians introduce us to a world where all is glowing with a gem-like lucency and distinctness.

"Decorative," no doubt, is the epithet that springs to our minds. Can this art ever be more than decorative? One might suppose that the interdict by Islam on representative art had driven the pictorial genius of the Persians into the designing of carpets and brocades, and tiles and vases; and it may well be that greater gifts were devoted to these in consequence than in other countries. The truth is that one passes from one of the great carpets to a painting without any feeling of crossing a border-line.

Yet a painting like that reproduced on Plate 35 — a page from a manuscript of the poems of Hafiz — leads one to think that had these painters enjoyed the opportunity, they could have made monumental designs for walls on a grand scale. This page in the original is not more than three inches high, yet it produces a sense of great bigness and stateliness. Again, a fifteenth-century painting.

But what I want to show you is the way in which, within a framework of conventions that remains ingenuously simple, Persian painting gradually rose to a height and achieved a splendour peculiar to itself. This could not have happened without the activity of individual genius. Bihzad, the most famous of Persian painters, was working at Herat during the second half of this fifteenth century, and there were other masters hardly less gifted than he. If we look at miniatures dating from the middle of the fifteenth century or a little before, such as those in the Shah-namah belonging to the Royal Asiatic Society,[1] we see that Bihzad did

[1] Published by J. V. S. Wilkinson, India Society, London, 1931.

not attempt to alter the recognized scheme of pictorial tradition.

We have already noted certain marked differences between Persian and Chinese design; but the greatest difference of all is the conception of space. You can enter a Chinese painting in imagination with the feeling that you would be able to walk on and on without coming to an end. With a Persian painting it is quite different. You can enter into it, but you soon feel that you have reached the limit of what the artist has intended you to see. He has arranged an enclosed space, as the theatre in which the action is presented, and you must not trespass behind the scenes.

The analogy of the theatre is rather close; for it is human beings and human action that interest the Persians. They have no passion, like the Chinese, for great spaces and solitudes where the winds blow out of far horizons. For them, as for European artists, man is the centre and dominates the stage. And running through Persian art is a lively sense of drama.

There has been much dispute among critics as to what, among the many paintings attributed to Bihzad, are really works by his hand. The miniature in the British Museum reproduced on Plate 36 is one of those about which we can be fairly certain. When we compare this page with the painting of preceding times, we cannot but feel that here is something new. There is an extraordinary delicacy and sensitive sureness in the line, and rare beauty of colour; but the marvel is that this delicacy is combined with a very masculine force and vigour. How alive in every nerve are the riders and the camels which they ride! But above all there is a masterly inventiveness of design. There is a thrilling sense of combat, of hurt and shock, and yet there is nothing restless in the scene.

The same sense of drama, of a number of living beings, each different, each intent on what he is doing, is manifest in the paintings in a manuscript of the "Life of Timur" belonging to Mr. Robert Garrett of Baltimore.[1] One page pictures the building of a mosque at Samarcand under the impatient orders of Timur. The composition is extremely complicated and alive in all its parts, which are cunningly woven, with contrasts of curve against straight line and angle, into a stimulating pattern. This is the work of an original genius and creator. This and the

[1] Published by Sir Thomas Arnold, with reproductions in colour of all the miniatures. Quaritch, London, 1930.

other paintings in the book have always been attributed to Bihzad, though questioned by some modern critics. If they are not by him, one can only say: So much the worse for Bihzad.

A manuscript of Sadi's "Bustan" now in the Egyptian Library at Cairo contains what are perhaps the best-attested paintings of Bihzad. One of the pages is specially remarkable (Pl. 37). King Dara mistakes his herdsman for an enemy, and is drawing his bow, when the herdsman reproves him for his ignorance of his own servants. Here, as elsewhere, Bihzad delights us with unexpected inventions in design. The composition seems rather haphazard; in the horses especially he seems to be intent just on seizing their natural attitudes and movements; and yet there is a subtle rightness in the relation of each part to the whole. Bihzad accepts the conventions, the general idea of picture-making, gradually formed, as we have seen, by tradition; but within that framework what a fullness of life, what animation, what drama, he is able to create!

Can this art be carried further on its own traditional lines? We may well ask. There is a change, a development, in the sixteenth century, but it is an intensification of inherited qualities rather than a breaking of fresh ground.

As I said just now, the Persians have no passion for solitude and great spaces, like the
Chinese. And they developed no art of pure
landscape, like the landscape of Sung, where
the scene portrayed is, over and above what
the painter represents, a mirror of his mind or
mood.

Such a landscape as the sixteenth-century
drawing probably by Muhammadi, in the
Louvre, is exceptional. The line-drawing is exquisite; but the space is enclosed, and the interest is in the work of the fields, the dealings of
man with nature rather than nature herself. In
other paintings we find a favourite motive,
picnickers among the bare hills by the side of
rivulets bordered by iris and mallow and narcis-
sus; idylls conceived somewhat in the mood of
Giorgione and his followers in Venice. (Pl. 38.)

And yet when we contemplate some of the
backgrounds to scenes of romance and adventure, we feel that these painters might have
created a landscape art such as no other school
has invented: landscapes of fairyland, with fantastic rocks, flame-coloured crags, towering
precipices; strange harmonies of delicate and
indescribable tints, such as you might find in
the plumage of rare birds or sea-shells, com-

129

bined into a radiant pattern. No other art surely, not even that of the modern Impressionists, gives so full a sense of the splendour of the sunlight and the poignant beauty of the spring blossoms seen against the pure blue of the sky.

The most splendid of sixteenth-century manuscripts is the "Poems of Nizami" in the British Museum, dating from 1539 to 1543 A.D. The paintings [1] are by the most distinguished of the masters who came immediately after Bihzad.

Among the paintings in this manuscript is one which is peculiar in its subject; it portrays the Ascent of the Prophet on a starry night to the Seventh Heaven (Pl. 39).

It need hardly be said that, in view of the orthodox condemnation of painting, there are no religious paintings in the stricter sense of the word; I mean, paintings made to assist the mood of devotion. Illustrations of sacred story are, however, not infrequent. There are subjects from the Old Testament and from the life of Jesus.[2] And this subject, the Ascent of Muhammad to Heaven, has been painted over and over again, though never with such triumphant

[1] All reproduced in colour in *The Poems of Nizami*, described by L. Binyon. London, 1928.
[2] See *Painting in Islam*, by Sir Thomas Arnold, Oxford, 1928.

splendour as in this page. It is not the apotheosis
of the Prophet; it is an event in his earthly life;
he rode up to heaven and communed with God
and descended again to earth in the space of a
single night. But we can divine that, had these
painters enjoyed the scope and opportunity
denied them by Islam, they might have rivalled
the religious art of other countries.

A thrilling sense of ethereal motion pervades
the design: we seem to be lifted up in air as we
look at it. The Prophet, mounted on Buraq, the
steed of Paradise, rides up into the profound
blue of the night. From his person streams a
fiery radiance shredded off in little leaping
flames. The archangel Gabriel precedes him;
angels from all quarters of the sky float round,
bearing offerings of jewels and of heavenly
fruits, or swinging censers as they mount
through the curled white clouds, among which,
far below, swims the dwindled earth.

There is sublimity of conception here; yet if we
compare this glowing page with masterpieces of
East or West in which the mood of devotion has
found perfect expression — early Japanese pictures of Amida descending with angels from
heaven, or pictures of Sienese masters like Sas-
setta — do we not feel a certain trace of earthly

131

voluptuousness? The rhythms of the design are on a smaller scale. Nevertheless it is a magnificent vision.

Most of the work of Persian artists was done to illustrate poetry. Now "the best part of medieval Persian poetry," says a great authority, "is either genuinely mystical or so saturated with mysticism that it will never be more than half-understood by those who read it literally." The passion of the lover for his beloved, the symbolism of the wine-cup, are used to typify the longing of the soul for God, the intoxication of the soul with the divinity. This symbolism may be present when it would never be suspected from outside. I think it may well have been in the mind of Nizami when he wrote afresh the Arab story of Laila and Majnun. Majnun is made mad by his love, which is returned by Laila but thwarted by circumstance: he flees into the desert, and the wild animals come round him and make friends of him, as you see in the painting reproduced (Pl. 40). Laila has been married to another, against her will. After a time, her husband dies. She fulfils the prescribed period of mourning. At last the lovers are free. Laila goes out into the desert. After all their years of suffering, she and Majnun meet.

But alas! for them there is no joy of fulfilment. Majnun has lived in his dream so long that he is no more at home in this world. The ideal has killed the real. His frenzy returns upon him and he rushes away from his beloved. Can it be that the strange composition with its endless curves and total absence of a straight line may consciously or unconsciously have symbolized for the artist the labyrinth of fate, with no earthly outlet, in which Majnun is entangled?

Or is that too fanciful a suggestion? At any rate, as one turns over the pages of this manuscript, one may well think that this pictorial art, where the lustrous colours in their pure intensity have been combined, as nowhere else in the world, into perfect harmony, is an art peculiarly apt for expressing a certain strain of mystical feeling. The colour goes to the head like wine. It can be literally intoxicating.

We may find nothing but an exquisite appeal to the senses in such a picture as that of the musician playing to Khosru in his court, or in other pages where Khosru comes upon Shirin bathing in a pool in the wilderness, or where Bahram, "that great hunter," pursues the wild ass among the golden sands of the desert, while the beautiful Azada plays to him on her harp.

But at least in all of these pages it is no gross transcript of everyday vision, it is an almost dazzling revelation of a world washed clean, where every object glows like pebbles in transparent water and is made precious to the eye.

In the picture of Nushirwan the Sasanian king, known to us as Chosroes I, coming with his Vizier upon a village ruined and deserted through the costly wars the king was always waging, though the scene is one of desolation, everything is distinct and gem-like in distinctness: the young deer feeding inside the ruin, the storks in their nest on the roof, high against a sky of gold dappled with blue and white cloud, the iris and mallow flowers by the stream, the defaced building, the broken tiles. This painting is by Mirak, second in fame only to Bihzad.

You may look on these paintings just as gorgeous illustrations to poetry. But when we pass to painting in which the religious feeling I have spoken of is explicit, we see how naturally akin already is the vision of these painters to the vision of the Sufi poets.

On a summer night, driving in an automobile, have you not sometimes been startled and thrilled by the apparition of wayside flowers and grasses suddenly isolated and luminous in

the beams of the headlamps? A moment ago
there was darkness; now with each stem and
leaf and petal delicately distinct, they seem to
have something unearthly in their beauty. Can
they really have been there in the dark, with all
that intricate profusion of form and colour?
You feel as if they had suddenly been created for
you yourself.

This may be an experience that passes and is
forgotten. But for some natures with a bent or
a gift for mysticism, such experiences are not
exceptional but habitual.

In our own day this peculiar vein of feeling is
present, I think, in the paintings of Vincent Van
Gogh; for him not only sunflower and iris but a
straw-bottomed chair, a pair of old boots, could
be illuminated with a light that never was, en-
riching not only the senses but the inward eye.

I showed you in my last lecture a Chinese
picture of a Buddhist mystic, a woman, straying
on a forlorn shore in the dead of winter, seeking
for the Absolute in essential solitude.

Very different externally, yet essentially akin,
is the Persian poet (Pl. 41) among the spring
flowers in their incredible beauty. The one is
for immersing herself in "the world wherein
no creature dwelleth" (to use the phrase of

135

Boehme), the world within oneself; the other "sees the world in a grain of sand, and a heaven in a wild flower." An intoxication of the senses merges into an intoxication of the spirit.

If I may illustrate from another English poet, that merging is visible in Marvell's "Thoughts in a Garden," where, at first entranced and ensnared among the voluptuous fruits and scented flowers, he soon passes into a deeper experience;

> the mind from pleasure less
> Retires into its happiness
>
> .   .   .   .
>
> Annihilating all that's made
> To a green thought in a green shade.

That painting, though assuredly painted by a Persian, was made in India; for the Persian miniatures were to become the classics of the art for the painters of the Moghul court at Delhi and Agra.

Babur, the first of the Moghul emperors, invaded India and conquered a large territory, but he died before he could consolidate his empire. His son Humayun could not keep his throne; he was driven out and spent long years in exile. One year was spent at the Persian court at Tabriz, and two young painters whom he met there were persuaded to join him later in Afghanistan and to follow him into India when at last he regained his throne.

So the Persian style passes into Indian painting.

We left the story of Indian painting at the close of the Buddhist period, with the latest of the Ajanta frescoes, about the seventh century. What had happened, what had been produced, in the intervening centuries? We are confronted with an almost total blank. No doubt there had been immense destruction by Muhammadans; still, it seems very strange that a few fragments of fresco and a few paintings in manuscripts should be all there is to represent the pictorial art of a thousand years.

What we note is that the rare Hindu paintings of the time of Akbar show no trace at all of that plastic sense which we found at Ajanta and Bagh; on the contrary the painting is flat, and the hieratic conventions seem to point back to some remotely primitive epoch, more antique than any of the Buddhist frescoes.

On the other hand, in the paintings of the Moghul school we find traces of a quite different tendency. It is true that Persian art provided the classic models for the painters at the court of Akbar and his son Jahangir; but it seems to me that in the end it was European art which had more influence than Persian on the Moghul style. The Jesuits brought to India engravings of religious subjects, mostly by Italianized Flemings and Dutchmen. Poor things, no doubt, but they had the European feeling for the third dimension and for atmosphere; and this had the charm of novelty.

Now when the Jesuits brought European oil-paintings to China and showed portraits with one half of the face, as the convention then was, in strong shadow, the Chinese were completely puzzled. "Do your friends then," they asked, "wash only one side of the face?" So used were they to their own conventions, that they simply did not *see* shadow. And they did not like its representation.

The Indians, however, seem to have been rather attracted by effects of light and shade; a favourite Moghul subject will be a group of ascetics sitting round a fire at night, or it may be hunters hunting deer with lanterns. It is all rather tentative, and there is no attempt to master the Western manner. The sort of compromise arrived at may be illustrated in a well-known painting in the British Museum of the Emperor Shah Jahan visiting a religious teacher in his hut, while the immemorial life of the Indian fields goes on around them (Pl. 42). The pure lustrous colouring of Persia has gone. We are conscious of a divided aim, though in its way the painting has real beauty.

In many Moghul paintings, of course, there is no attempt to represent the effect of atmosphere, and the colouring, though not so radiant as the Persian, is attractive in its harmonies.

The strength of the school is in portraiture. Portraits are rare in Persian art. But the Moghul painters excel in rendering the features of the Emperors and the nobles and officers, so varied in race and type, who thronged the imperial court. Jahangir, who passed for a great patron of art, delighted in his painters' skill and was interested in the documentary side of painting, but not at all, I think, in the creative side. It was characteristic of him to order an artist to portray a victim of opium when he was dying; the man was in fact dead the day after the painting, now in the Bodleian Library at Oxford, was made. (Pl. 43.)

Meanwhile the Hindu artists who worked at small courts, away from the centre of the Empire, especially those who worked in the valleys of the Himalayas, were creating an art which

139

was truly Indian, though it may well be that
Persian example had taught these painters
something of the suavity and flow which is the
special charm of their line-drawing. There is a
famous line-drawing of a camel and groom by
a sixteenth-century Persian master (Pl. 44).
The line is what is called calligraphic; the
strokes in themselves, and apart from the forms
they enclose, apart from the element of representation, have a peculiar beauty. They communicate a physical thrill. And yet what could
be more satisfying as draughtsmanship? How
perfectly the forms are evoked! There is complete equilibrium. In later drawings the calligraphic element is in excess. We are too conscious of the artist's delight in his own skill;
the lines become part of a pattern, they do not
create an image.

Now look at an Indian Rajput drawing of two
lovers in a pavilion hailing the moonrise over a
lake (Pl. 45). It is more tentative in execution
because intended to be coloured. The quality
of the line is near akin to the Persian, and yet
we feel a difference. It is conceived in a different mood; and the character of the line is gov-
erned by the mood, the lyrical mood, of the
drawing. The line flows over all the accidents

of form like a stream, and refuses to be impeded by them. The gesture of the lovers as they watch the flight of herons over the lake, the movement of the attendant maids who fan them and play music to them — every form and movement in the design melts naturally into the spontaneous rhythm that controls the whole. You feel the artist's joy in the tracing of his lines just for their own sake; yet this is fused with the joy that overflows and radiates from the whole design.

Many a Western artist would try to express that joy merely through the faces of the lovers. Here every line is eloquent. Is there anything in the art of the world so like a song that sings itself?

PLATE 28

BRONZE IBEX. PERSIA, ACHAEMENID DYNASTY

PLATE 29

MONKEY RIDING A TURTLE, AN ILLUSTRATION TO "THE
FABLES OF BIDPAY." PERSIA, EARLY

MONKEY THROWING FIGS TO A TURTLE, AN ILLUSTRATION
TO "THE FABLES OF BIDPAY." PERSIA

PLATE 30

PAGE FROM SHAH-NAMAH BY FIRDAUSI. PERSIA, 11TH CENTURY

PLATE 31

PAGE FROM SHAH-NAMAH BY FIRDAUSI. PERSIA, 11TH CENTURY

PLATE 32

DUEL. PERSIA, TIMURID, DATED 1396 A.D.

PLATE 33

NIGHT SCENE IN A GARDEN. PERSIA, TIMURID,
DATED 1396 A.D.

PLATE 34

PRINCE HUMAY AND PRINCESS HUMAYUN. PERSIA, 15TH CENTURY

PLATE 35

THREE LADIES, AN ILLUSTRATION TO THE POEMS
OF HAFIZ. PERSIA, 15TH CENTURY

PLATE 36

FIGHT ON CAMELBACK, BY BIHZAD. PERSIA, 15TH CENTURY

PLATE 37

KING DARA AND THE HERDSMAN, BY BIHZAD. PERSIA, 15TH CENTURY

PLATE 38

PASTORAL LANDSCAPE, BY MUHAMMADI.
PERSIA, 16TH CENTURY.

PLATE 39

ASCENT OF THE PROPHET. PERSIA, 16TH CENTURY

PLATE 40

MAJNUN AND THE BEASTS.   PERSIA, 16TH CENTURY

PLATE 41

MULLAH AMONG FLOWERS.   INDIA, MOGHUL,
17TH CENTURY

PLATE 42

SHAH JAHAN VISITING HIS MULLAH. INDIA, MOGHUL,
17TH CENTURY

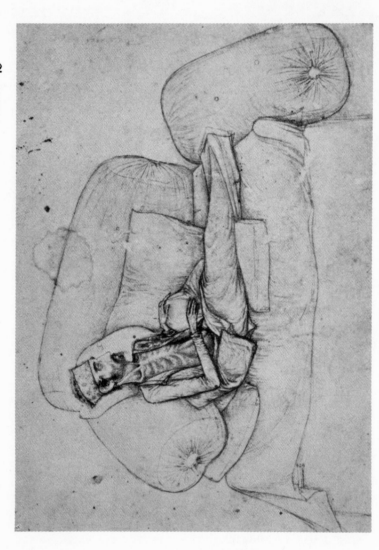

PLATE 43

DRAWING OF A DYING MAN FOR A PAINTING IN THE BODLEIAN
LIBRARY, OXFORD. INDIA, MOGHUL

PLATE 44

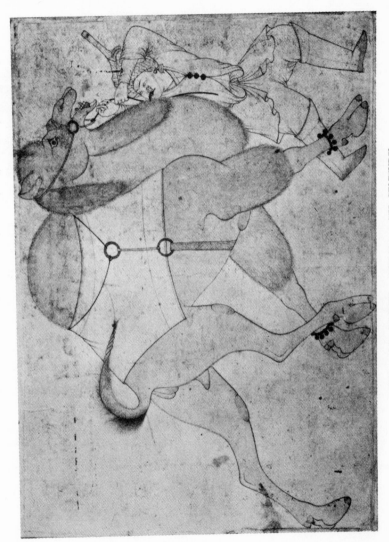

CAMEL AND DRIVER. PERSIA, 16TH CENTURY

PLATE 45

LOVERS IN A PAVILION. INDIA. RAJPUT

Lecture V

JAPANESE ART

IN THE precinct of a temple on the outskirts
of Kyoto there is a garden designed by a
famous artist of the fifteenth century, Soami. It
is called a garden; but anything less like our
notion of a garden could hardly be conceived.
Imagine a long rectangle bordered by a low curb
of stone and filled with an expanse of finest
sand, raked every morning into a rippling pattern of waves. Not a flower, not a shrub, not a
blade of grass; only that silvery surface, and
emerging from it in a quite unsymmetrical group
four or five small rocks of irregular shape. What
was in the mind of the designer of this strange
garden, or ghost of a garden, so bare, so devoid
of all the sensuous charms we seek for in the
colour and perfume of flowers, the smoothness
of lawns, the shade of trees?

We can only guess; but we may be sure that
this garden was conceived in the spirit of Zen,
the sect of contemplation. We have already
seen how this sect of Buddhism, with its denial
of the value of rites and ceremonies, and of the
reading of the scriptures, with its quest of the
Absolute in the depths of the individual heart,

143

came to tinge the art of China in the period of Southern Sung. And in the fifteenth century it took such possession of the Japanese spirit that the art of the Ashikaga period is even more deeply impregnated with Zen than was the art of Sung before it.

That singular garden of Soami's, with its nakedness, its abstraction, shows the Zen spirit in an extreme form. In the art inspired by Zen all the emphasis is on the interior life, and the communication of ideas is reduced to the simplest, barest forms. It is an art of suggestion rather than expression.

I shall return to that phase of Japan's art. But at the outset I should like to dwell for a moment on this propensity to carry things to extremity, to sacrifice everything else to the chosen aim, which I think is characteristic of the race and which sometimes will appear to us almost fantastic, almost terrifying.

Okakura has observed that the strong element of common sense in the Chinese nature has prevented the Chinese from carrying things to extremes in the world of ideas and the world of action. In this respect, he says, the Japanese are much nearer to the Indians.

Among the Indian stories of Buddha's in-

carnations before his appearance as the Sakya-
muni of history, there is one which tells how as
a Brahmin he went on a journey with his wife,
and how on his way first one and then others
whom he meets ask him for his various posses-
sions. He gives them, one by one, to those who
desire them, and when he has given them all
away, someone asks him for his wife. He gives
her away, too, without resistance or demur. He
was carrying out an idea to the very end.

Now there is a story of a Japanese woman
weeping on a battlefield over the bodies of her
dead sons; to someone who sought to comfort
her she replied: "I do not weep because I have
lost them, I weep because I have no more sons
to give." The story of the Forty-Seven Ronin
is known, I expect, to many of you — the story
of the forty-seven retainers, who, to avenge
their feudal lord, conspired to kill the enemy who
had wronged him, and then committed suicide.
This, one would think, was enough. But in some
cases these men had widowed mothers whom it
would have been a crime to abandon in their
old age. These mothers hanged themselves of
their own accord in order that the duty of filial
piety might not interfere with the duty of loyalty
to the feudal lord. This is a true story. The

145

graves of these men are in a temple in Tokyo, and whatever day you visit it there will be sticks of incense burning before each grave and crowds thronging the temple. These crowds come to the temple, not to pray for benefits to themselves, but merely to pay homage to an act of loyalty and courage performed more than two centuries ago.

There is a sort of absolute quality in the Japanese loyalty to a cause or an idea. Probably in the history of the world there has never been a race so heroic, I mean so possessed by the spirit which is ready to dare all and endure all, regardless of consequence, in the cause which it has chosen. Though this spirit is manifested most strikingly in the world of action, it is present also in the world of ideas, and in art.

In Japanese art we are to look for no careless creative profusion, no copious magnificence; it is rather a fine distillation, a concentration of aim exerted in the direction of a fastidious delicacy of taste. Its weakness is, I think, not so much want of originality as too great a measure of consciousness in production and a seducing skill in execution.

The history of Japanese art is the history of an art which takes its first inspiration from

146

China, gradually develops a character of its own and takes on new subject-matter; then, as if in fear of losing touch with the great traditions of the Continent, of becoming provincial and insular, it seeks and finds a fresh invigoration and renewal from a later phase of Chinese art and thought. Again Japan shuts herself up; again her art sets itself to assimilate what it has absorbed; again a new style of truly Japanese character is gradually formed. There are later phases of the art in which something of the same kind occurs, but not to the same extent. What is so notable is that for well over a thousand years and down to our own day there is a continuous succession of artists in every generation; and if their gifts differ in scope and quality, if one phase is richer than another, there is no barren and no stagnant period.

Let us place ourselves in Japan, let us imagine what sort of mental atmosphere we should absorb and grow up in were we born in that island empire; I do not mean today, but in the times before Japan had any knowledge of Europe and the West.

I was told the other day of a Chinese pioneer student who came to America, I think in the 1870's, and who said that till he came to this country he had never heard the names of Rome, Athens, or Jerusalem. It requires an effort for us to realize that a man should be in a state of what we are accustomed to regard as lamentable ignorance, and yet be highly cultured and refined. The Japanese would be in this case, but they would have behind them the great background of China, and with Chinese thought and art would be inseparably mingled the heritage of Indian philosophy and religion flowing into China and Korea through Buddhism. There on the vast mainland — all they knew of the world outside their islands — were their Rome, their Athens, their Jerusalem.

It is a current fashion to decry the Japanese as a nation of mere imitators. Should we praise the Northern nations of Europe for their originality if they had stubbornly rejected instead of ardently embracing the art and thought and literature of the Mediterranean? We should not. Like those Northern nations, Japan had the sense to recognize, when she saw it, a superior civilization; in either case it embodied the best that the spirit of man had achieved within their knowledge, and Japan adopted the heritage of China with gratitude and enthusiasm.

I remember years ago receiving a visit from

148

an old Japanese scholar, who looked, with his parchment face and austere yet mild expression, like those portraits of Buddhist monks that the older masters of Japan have painted. He had seen the gifts of Western civilization to his country, the machines, the inventions, the devices of comfort and luxury; and he had come on a pilgrimage to the West because he could not believe that it had not something better to offer — some way of life, some ideal. We to-day speak of Japan as transformed by the adoption of our civilization, but I should conjecture (though I may be mistaken) that such transformation as there is affects the appearance more than the essence; that it is largely external.

It was different with the change that came over Japan in the sixth and seventh centuries, when Chinese culture was so eagerly and so thoroughly absorbed. That was a real transformation: its primary effect was not on externals, but on the mind and spirit. The art and culture of China came to Japan in the wake of Buddhism. The movement had behind it all the momentum of religious fervour.

It was the Crown Prince Shotoku, who died in 621 A.D., to whom, far more than any other, the introduction of Buddhism, and Confucian-ism, and the arts and graces of life, was due. His is one of the greatest names of Japanese history.

The surviving relics of the art of this period are almost all sculpture, but among them are statues hardly excelled anywhere for the felicity with which they express a spiritual conception. Buddhism came to Japan through Korea, but Korean and Japanese sculptors alike modelled their style on that of the Chinese style of a little earlier time, the style of Northern Wei.

The wooden statue of Kwannon, the Bodhisattva of Compassion, reproduced on Plate 46, dates from Shotoku's time. The instinct of the artist has led him to prolong the flowing lines, to attenuate the body, just as we find in some of the Gothic statues on European cathedrals, or in the paintings of El Greco and Blake — wherever the idea of spiritual rather than corporeal presence is dominant. The extended hand adds by its gesture an extraordinary tenderness.

When I was in Japan, this statue seemed to me so entrancing that I approached Mr. Niiro, a famous and marvellous craftsman and restorer, with a view to having a facsimile of it for the British Museum. Its delivery was long delayed. We heard that no suitable camphor tree could be found, and it had to be made of camphor wood, like the original. At last a prince offered a majestic tree in his grounds for the purpose, and a religious service was held before the tree, and pardon was asked for cutting it down, as it was to become a divine image.

Even finer as sculpture, in its combination of breadth and subtlety, and more expressive of feature, is the seated Kwannon at a nunnery near Nara (Pl. 47).

There are various types of Bodhisattvas belonging to this period; and one favourite type is seated in the attitude of Rodin's "Penseur." But instead of a massive form which appears to be masticating an unpalatable thought with a kind of animal bewilderment, we have forms of exquisitely slender mould, the chin just resting on the finger-tips, half-smiling and as if lost in peace.

Nara was now the capital; it was transformed from a small town into a splendid city. Shrunken again today to a fraction of its former size, Nara, with its ancient temples and the deer that stray about its open parks, is still a city of enchantment. There is the Sho-so-in, the treasure-house dedicated in the eighth century to Buddha. A primitive wooden structure, it contains all the personal belongings of an emperor. It is opened once a year for a few days in November, and the sun shines in upon the musical instruments, screens, swords, writing materials, chess-boards, incense-burners, used in that far-off time. All are of exquisite workmanship. Chinese design predominates. Persian art is also represented. One has a momentary vision of what all that wondrous inheritance from the Asian continent must have meant to this youthful and susceptible nation destined to be the ultimate recipient of it: all the art, and thought, and ceremony, and legend, the rich Chinese tissue with threads woven into it from Greece and the Mediterranean as well as from India and Iran. That they were not overwhelmed by these sudden riches, but could adapt and absorb and finally re-create in a new style, is a testimony to the patience, the thoroughness, the assimilative genius, of the Japanese.

The bronze trinity in Horyuji (Pl. 48) is of a little later date. Amida Buddha, the Lord of Light, is in the centre and a Bodhisattva is on either side of him. Each is seated on the lotus, the flower which springs from the mud to unfold its stainless petals above the water, just as the soul has need of the gross passions of earth from which to rise, by its own impulse and effort, into passionless serenity. It is a masterpiece of workmanship, and of the Buddhist style, unrivalled in its consummate delicacy by anything of the kind surviving in China. Of especial beauty is the decoration of the screen behind the figures. The springing curves in low relief create an illusion of movement, like the wavering lines of smoke ascending in the air, and give strange life to the celestial beings who seem to rise on their lotus thrones from unseen water below.

The early Buddhist art of Japan has indeed a peculiar and rare quality and is worth attentive study, such as Mr. and Mrs. Langdon Warner have devoted to it in their exhaustive work on Suiko sculpture. The Japanese style is in gradual process of formation. In general we may say that the tendency is to refine on the Chinese style, to achieve a still more fastidious delicacy and sensitiveness. Contrast the coarsening touch of the Romans in their imitation of Greek marbles. To the completeness of assimilation there is something added, so that what emerges has a personal character and flavour.

Most of the earliest paintings have perished. It is in the tenth century that we come to a remarkable group of religious pictures associated

with the name of a priest called Eshin. A dream
of the moonrise is said to have inspired the
painter's vision of the glorified Buddha rising
behind the mountains. In this art, the design
and the workmanship alike are such as to communicate with supreme felicity the sense of unearthliness and of a living peace. To the same
school belongs a pair of paintings picturing
Amida Buddha descending with angels to wel-
come the blest. All white and gold on dim blue,
these ethereal forms floating in the air seem to
move to the strains of music (Pl. 49).

It was in this period, the end of the tenth
century, that a woman, Lady Murasaki, wrote
the greatest of Japanese (and doubtless of all
Oriental) novels, *The Tale of Genji*, now beginning to be well known in the West through
Mr. Waley's beautiful translation.

The earliest illustrations to *Genji* surviving
are of the twelfth century, and they are some of
the earliest works in the school of purely Japanese style which was gradually forming. The
horizontal scrolls of this school were unlike anything Chinese. We look down upon palace
verandahs, or into interiors with their screened
apartments; there may be a delicate painting
of flowers or grasses on a sliding panel, but there

154

is no furniture, unless we can say that the figures themselves are the furniture; for the young prince and the ladies he converses with are so enveloped in voluminous dresses that they seem incapable of any but the most ceremonious movements and have the look almost of precious objects arranged in a decorative scheme.

The formal design that results is curiously fascinating, and we meet strange colour-harmonies unknown to the art of Europe. Straight line and angle play far more part in the design than with the Chinese painters. (Pl. 50.)

This art is the reflection of a period which has no parallel elsewhere in history. The Japanese propensity to carry things to extremity is seen in an attempt to order life by a purely aesthetic ideal. If beauty, they seem to say, is the most precious thing in the world, let us believe in it, let us take it for our star and guide, and go to the very end.

Never was devotee more exacting with himself, never was moralist more exacting with other people, in pursuit of the right. But it was not right belief or right conduct that was the standard; it was right taste. Art dominated life. A noble addressed a lady with a little poem, which he handed to her on a fan. It was her duty to respond at once with a poem in answer. And the poem's essence lay in what it did not say, in what it subtly suggested. An inelegance in the handwriting, the choice of an inferior kind of paper, was the gravest of solecisms.

Once a lady appeared at a court function in a dress which had a little fault in the colour combination at the wrist opening. It was noticed at once by the whole court, and cost the lady bitter tears. The authoress of *The Tale of Genji* records the incident in her diary and adds, "It was not so bad; only one colour was a little too pale." As Miss Amy Lowell comments,[1] that little incident illuminates a whole era.

Yet human nature will not be denied, and to read *The Tale of Genji* is to discover what a delicate fabric of human relationships, what tremblings of the heart, and even what sighings after the world of the spirit lay beneath this gorgeous stiff brocade of existence, where choice shades of colour counted for so much.

And indeed, though the painting of these court scenes was soon to become frozen into formula, in the earliest and finest of the illustrations to *Genji* we can feel a tremulousness

[1] *Diaries of Court Ladies.* Translated by Annie S. Omori and Kochi Doi, Boston, 1920.

of contained emotion even in the strokes
of the brush, though so little is seen on the
surface.

It is thus that in the No play of later times,
so highly abstract in its way of representing
action, we are made to feel how tremendous a
pressure of emotion is hidden beneath the stiff
conventions, just as the features of the actors
are hidden beneath the subtly moulded masks
they wear.

Nothing in *The Tale of Genji* is more remarkable than the singular susceptibility to the
beauty of nature shown by these lords and
ladies whose lives seem more ceremonious and
artificial than life at the court of Louis Quatorze
or Louis Quinze. Numberless little phrases of
description by the way — white flowers seen
over a fence with petals half-unfolded "like the
lips of people smiling at their own thoughts,"
the "almost unbearable beauty" of a scene at
night when someone was singing under the
moonlit trees — tell of a sensibility that is all
the more astonishing when we see the impassive
features portrayed in the paintings.

This life with all its strange elaborated beauty
as of some great orchid blossom, exotic in its
form, exquisite in its colour, subtle in its pur-

157

pose, could not last. It was to be rudely over-thrown.

But even before the great clash of warrior clans begins, and the long civil wars ensue which are to bring such misery and devastation, there appears an artist who reveals a vein of humour and vivacity truly characteristic of the Japanese genius, yet strongly contrasting with the scenes of court life and courtly romance.

Japan was now closed to all foreign inter-course, and, shut in upon herself, was evolving an art independent of Chinese models. Now we find pages from the actual life of the day, a scene at a cock-fight, games and wrestlers, the rough-and-tumble of the streets. Who is this artist who is master of so nervous a brush-line, of so summary a means of expression? It is, strange to say, an archbishop of the Buddhist church. Perhaps a venerable dignitary, but with what a sense of fun! He loves to caricature his clergy, slyly exhibiting their sleek pomposity or ineptitude in the guise of blinking frogs and timid hares and mischievous monkeys.

How fresh the drawings are! They might have been made today. Toba Sojo is the father of Japanese caricature. But he is more than a caricaturist. He painted religious subjects also. And in his famous drawing of fighting bulls one feels the hand of a great artist. (Pl. 51.)

These bulls might well symbolize the terrific struggle about to begin between the two clans of Taira and Minamoto. They contended for the person of the Emperor; and when the Taira forces had been at last exterminated, Yoritomo made himself dictator under the name of Shogun. The Emperor, though treated as a sacred personage, lost all reality of power, which remained in the hands of successive dynasties of Shoguns till 1868.

The capital was moved to Kamakura, after which city this epoch is named.

This age of civil war is full of tragic and heroic episodes. The story of Kumagaye, the hard old warrior who at the great battle on the shores of the Inland Sea pursued the sixteen-year-old Atsumori into the waves and overpowered and killed him, and then, pursued by remorse and haunted by the young beauty of the boy's head, revealed when his helmet was struck off, shaved his head and became a monk — that story is typical of the time. We are reminded of the Middle Ages of Europe with their unending wars, and the extravagant exploits of the knights,

159

and the numberless monasteries in which learning and art were kept alive.

Even the Buddhist sculpture now changes its
character and assumes, instead of the earlier
slenderness and sweetness, a massive force and
power.

It was Japan's age of chivalry. How striking
a contrast with China, where reverence has ever
been given to the scholar, but the soldier has
ranked with the lowest of the low!

That Japan has had her age of chivalry is
something which, if we would understand the
Japanese, should never be forgotten. With this
age of Kamakura, art assumes a new and virile
form. The typical paintings of the period are
long horizontal scrolls, *makimono*, presenting
scenes of battle and adventure, journeys, legends, lives of saints.

It is above all in the scenes of war that these
painters excel. For the most part it is in scenes
from the civil war, but there are also rolls depicting the attempted invasion of Japan by the
Mongols, fierce outlandish warriors, contrasted
with the armoured knights of Japan. There are
skirmishes on the seashore; groups of soldiers
waiting for orders, generals in council; horsemen reconnoitring in the pine-woods. A tense

excitement is visible not only in the faces, but in the attitudes, in the whole atmosphere. (Pl. 52.)

To show sections or extracts only, which is all one can do, is to do injustice to the narrative character of the painting, for which the form of the long roll was admirably adapted. In the West we have no such means of telling a story pictorially. We cannot, as in these rolls, exhibit the progress and sequence of events; and our illustrations of history suffer from the effort to compress more than is reasonable into a given space, and at the same time make a satisfying composition; for the painter is confined to a single moment. Critics nowadays are shocked at the idea of a picture telling a story. But if a story can be presented pictorially, even more vividly than by words, why in the world shouldn't it?

Certainly in the representation of action the Japanese are in their element. What masculine force they put into the brush-line! There is a tensity of expectation in these scenes of war which is of the essence of drama. (Pl. 53.)

In the famous roll at Boston, the "Flight of the Court," the mad rush of the ox-drawn chariots, the headlong movement, are given with marvellous reality. And as the warriors set the palace on fire, the flames leap out, the wood cracks; we seem to feel the heat of the blaze, to hear the roar of it and the stamping of armed men.

These rolls, so little known to the West, are in some ways Japan's greatest contribution to the world's art. They are specifically Japanese. There are no battle-pictures to equal them. They reflect the soul of the Samurai, exulting in action, shrinking from no extreme of suffering in their cause.

To us, of course, they cannot have the same force of appeal as they have for the Japanese. What are nameless figures to us, are to them heroes familiar from childhood. Nor, as I said, can any justice be done to the rolls in mere sections or extracts. To get the narrative and dramatic quality inherent in the design, one must unroll them from beginning to end.

But it is not all battle and bloodshed, this age of trouble and warfare.

Koya-san is a sacred mountain, near Osaka, covered with forest trees. On the summit, among huge black pines, is a great graveyard, and in the midst of it is the tomb of the renowned saint Kobo, who lived in the early

162

ninth century. Lamps burn before it per-
petually.

Look at the ideal portrait of the saint as a boy,
seated praying upon the lotus, which is reproduced on Plate 54. All material things seem to
be melted away in the presence of this pure
image. It might so easily have been a mere
abstraction, but with all the purity of form it
is the portraiture of a living, breathing child.
It is at once remote and intimate.

These pictures were painted in a period of con-
flict and waste; of high drama and surpassing
heroism; but also of wide and enduring misery
for the people. There was no security from day
to day; all was uncertain and precarious. All
the more was there need for a permanent reality
of the spirit. Thought was turned inward. No
wonder, then, that the Zen doctrine, with its
denial of the reality of the material world and
its emphasis on the inner self, sank deep into
the minds of the Japanese, even of the warriors.
The Zen sect had found expression in the art of
the Sung age in China. Now with even greater
thoroughness, as we have seen already, it coloured and gave its special character to the art
of the Ashikaga period, the days of the Ashikaga
line of Shoguns, who ruled from the fourteenth

to the sixteenth century. We may surmise, indeed, that the painting of action and adventure, of battle and bloodshed, produced a reaction of weariness; that other and deeper elements of the human spirit craved for expression. And it may be, also, that there was an instinctive feeling that the Japanese spirit had become impoverished by long isolation; that it needed a fresh contact with the larger world of Asian culture.

At any rate, by the fifteenth century a new wave of Chinese influence was gathering impetus and was soon to flood the whole art of Japan.

We can imagine the scene when in the Golden Pavilion (still standing near Kyoto) the Shogun who had abdicated and the scholars and artists he had gathered round him opened reverentially some newly-arrived box containing a masterpiece of Sung painting by Ma Yüan or Mu Ch'i; just as Lorenzo de Medici would invite the artists of Florence to his palace to view some newly-discovered antique marble. Later, another of the Ashikaga rulers retired to the Silver Pavilion.

Liberation and self-enlightenment: that I conceive is the aim of Zen. Just as ceremony and the recital of the scriptures, and even (if necessary) the use of words, were renounced as of no value in themselves — for the aim was to keep the soul clear from the least creeping film that would cloud it, the least stagnation of habit — so art was to avoid the elaborate and ornate, as building up a sort of wall or barrier instead of letting the thought of the artist pass free and full with the mind of the beholder. A hint, a suggestion, sufficed.

Now was instituted the first tea-ceremony by the painter Soami. It was a school of taste, a philosophy of manners. The tea-room is a small chamber, quite bare; its proportions are all prescribed. A single picture is hung on the wall; and with it the host will show a bowl, which must be congruous in quality with the picture. The small pictures painted for the tea-ceremony are those most typical of this time and school.

I have already spoken of Soami's garden. We might perhaps find a clue to his conception in a little poem of the thirteenth century inspired by the Zen spirit and often associated with the ceremony:

> Out across the wave
> All is bare;
> Not a scarlet leaf,
> Not a flower there!
> Only over thatched huts falling brief
> Twilight, and the lonely autumn air.

Japanese gardens are not of course, as a rule, so uncompromising in reticent austerity as that which I described to you. But they are very differently conceived from our gardens. They appeal less to the senses and more to the mind. There are no beds glowing with many-coloured flowers, but the garden is designed to be a world in miniature; it should contain in little all the elements of great landscape: rocks and water, hills and trees; bridges over the water; winding paths that yield vistas as they wind.

You are familiar no doubt with those dwarf trees in pots which the Japanese so ingeniously rear, and perhaps you have dismissed them as mere freakish toys. But the intention behind them is the same as that behind the gardens. It is not a forcing of nature into an unnatural smallness; at least, that is not the point. Just as a man strolling in his garden may imagine himself among streams and great mountains, so, sitting in his room beside a dwarf pine-tree and retiring into his own inner mind, he may by intensity of contemplation become himself small as a midget while the tree dilates and towers, and soon he is translated to the solitude of the forest where the great branches extend far overhead and murmur in the wind.

The dwarf tree is not a toy, it is an instrument of contemplation. May I quote one of our own poets for comparison?

> And now to the abyss I pass
> Of the unfathomable grass,
> Where men like grasshoppers appear;
> But grasshoppers are giants there
> And from the precipices tall
> Of the green spires to us do call.

But this is by the way.

You may remember perhaps Walter Pater's imaginary portrait of Duke Carl of Rosenmold, the young German princeling, bred in the confinement of a little court among the pine-forests and rainy hills, who is possessed by a passionate nostalgia for the Greek world of light and liberation. To him the radiance of Apollo is transmitted but dimly and foggily, and at more than one remove. But even the echo of an echo which sounds through the French classicism of the eighteenth century still has power to enchant.

That story exemplifies the persistent desire of the human spirit to attune itself to some favoured epoch which seems to embody with special felicity a harmonization of life. In Europe it is the Periclean age in Athens that has above all others lured and charmed posterity.

In like manner the artists of the Ashikaga time strove to attune themselves to the Sung age in China. And they achieved their aim with astounding success. For the contemporary Chinese art, the art of the Ming dynasty, did not appeal to the Japanese of this time; splendid in its way, it was, so to speak, external in its beauty, it was not sympathetic. And no doubt the attunement to the Sung spirit was the more successful because the Sung period was over and closed, and represented a permanent achievement, not subject to change.

Now, instead of the glowing colours of the Yamato school, the painters charge their brushes with ink and sweep on to the silvery paper swift evocations of landscape, birds, or bamboo. It is the life of action exchanged for the life of contemplation.

These pictures are sometimes too slight to convey much to one who has no clue to the mental atmosphere from which they came. This is an esoteric art. Yet the slightness will never appear superficial. It is the miracle of art, as I have said before, that what is put into the work comes out from it. The full mind, the rich nature, makes itself felt in the tracing of a few vivid lines; the empty mind, the poor na-

168

ture, is betrayed in the most elaborate composition. (Pl. 56.)

This art of Ashikaga is above all a communication between mind and mind, a communication impossible to be expressed through language. Through the work of art the spectator
enters into the artist's spirit, and through that
into the universal life. Until this chain of relations is completed, the painting is in a sense
non-existent or only half-existent. Behind every
slight ink-sketch there is the significance of a
wave of thought inspiring a whole period.

Sesshu, indeed, the greatest master of the
time, not only suggests but creates. Even in
China, to which he journeyed, he was acclaimed
a master. His landscapes are painted with bold
and vehement strokes, though there is not the
same persuasion of reality that breathes in the
great landscapes of Sung. All this art indeed
has something of the same relation to the Sung
art as the drama of Corneille and Racine has
to the Greek drama. It is more formal, less
spontaneous, it avowedly follows a previous
model.

Though less typical of Sesshu's strong style,
there is a fascination about his conception of the
genius of old age peering out from among the

white blossoms of spring, while the mysterious fawn rubs its head against his knee. It is the romance of old age, richer than the romance of youth, because with all the experience of many years there is still preserved the sense of the wonder of the world. The conception is entirely Chinese. And in the art of this period there is little that is specifically Japanese in character, though it is not long before the native idiom asserts itself.

Once more, then, Chinese art and thought have flowed over Japan in a fertilizing stream. The old Yamato tradition of painting still lingers on, but the new Chinese manner has won the day and sets the vogue.

What will happen now? Will the two streams remain divided or will they coalesce?

Happily for Japan, they coalesced, at least in certain masters and certain styles. For the Yamato, the purely Japanese school, with its peculiar decorative conventions was petrifying into formula; and the schools which had developed their styles under the inspiration of the new movement from China had hardly sufficient interior life of their own to prevent a similar decline setting in before long. The most vigorous of these schools was the Kano school. The

later stages of this school, which has lasted till
our time, illustrate from the seventeenth century onward the progressive staleness, with in-
termittent recoveries, of an academic tradition.
We become as weary of the sages and storks,
the lakes and willows, the hills and streams of an
imaginary China, which the painters had never
seen, as we do in Europe of the Roman gods and
goddesses and nymphs and satyrs that sprawl
over ceilings to show off the painter's skill.

But already in the sixteenth century a new
note can be distinguished in some of the screen-
paintings of the Kano school.

Japanese screens are usually six-fold or two-
fold. They were often painted in ink, in the
Chinese manner. But the typical screen is on a
gold ground; more rarely, a silver ground. The
gold and silver were inherited from the Yamato
traditions, also the splendour of frank colour.

Among the early masters of the Kano school,
Motonobu, and still more his grandson Yeitoku,
painted magnificent screens.

The "Pines on Wintry Hills," in the Freer
collection (Pl. 57), is attributed to Yeitoku.
This is quite different from any Chinese landscape. It has not the depths of space to lure the
contemplative mind; it arrests us rather with

171

its solid forms, to stay on their simple massiveness. And although the design has a formal character, although the gold background precludes any study of atmosphere, the painter yet conveys to us a sharp feeling of the winter cold and the snow's brightness. There is no apparent symbolism, but somehow we are made conscious of a silent contending of invisible forces: the upward thrust of the pine-branches defies the heavy burden of the snow. It might be, I think, a congenial setting for a tragedy where the hero grandly contends with fate.

The chaos of civil strife and the rivalry of the great barons were at last put an end to by the low-born soldier of genius Hideyoshi, who conquered Korea and made himself master of Japan. With his ascendency taste changes; splendour is the note of the period, succeeding the reticent suggestion which the preceding period prized in art. When Hideyoshi made a progress, screens by Yeitoku and his pupils were set up on either side of the way for a mile on end. Yeitoku appears to have been the first to combine in his screen-paintings the decorative conventions and rich colour of the Yamato school with the synthetic treatment of the Chinese style. He had numerous followers.

172

A little later we come to a group of artists who carry this fusion of styles yet further, and in fact invent a new style, different from any that had gone before.

Koyetsu, the originator of the style, was a remarkable man. He was a painter and a calligrapher; his writing was even more prized than his painting. He made lacquer and pottery; he gave an impulse to wood-engraving. His aim was apparently something like that of William Morris, to refresh the traditional handicrafts with the inspiration of the artist. He was also an unrivalled connoisseur and an expert, especially on swords. Sword-making in Japan is a great art; swords by famous makers are priceless.

A beautiful screen in the Metropolitan Museum used to be thought to be by Koyetsu (Pl. 58). Whoever it was who painted it was a consummate artist. It is typical of the screen-painting of this group. The screens were a kind of wall-painting, and therefore it was essential that the effect of them should be decorative. They are indeed usually conceived of simply as fine decoration; that is a way of dismissing them. But all fine paintings are decorative to a greater or less degree, in so far as they

173

have rhythmical design. If in these screens the living forms of things were submerged in, and subdued to, the pattern of a design, then they might well be called simply decorative. But when the living forms, whether of figures, animals, trees, or flowers, are rendered with such intimacy and expressiveness that it is these rather than the pattern of design which one carries away in one's mind, then I think "decoration" is rather a meaningless label.

Walking in the woods of New Hampshire last October, when the leaves were in their glory, I could not help thinking that the pleasure one got from those burning colours and that tracery of trees could be perfectly communicated in art only by such a method as that of these screen-painters.

What realistic or impressionist picture could give us the quintessence of spring moonrise over a hillside, where the delicate flowers waver in the dim air, as does the screen painted on a silver ground which is reproduced on Plate 59? This is in the Freer collection and is ascribed to Sotatsu, the greatest painter in this little group of artists.

Taking a motive, or a few related motives, from the profusion of nature, these painters con-

174

centrate on their beauty and significance, enhancing each motive by a certain isolation from irrelevant surroundings. The Persians so enhance the particular beauty of flowers, magnifying their scale; but the flowers are set in what passes for a complete representation of a scene, and remain subordinate features. Here is that kind of distillation of the elements of a scene which I have suggested belongs to the special character of Japanese art.

The style was carried to a climax in the next generation by Korin. In the famous screen-painting of "Waves" at Boston, we feel as if the artist had brooded in his mind over the memory of the boiling and swirling waves among the islets of Matsushima, till the water had acquired a sort of ghostly life of its own and had appeared before him in a vision. The sinuous lines seem actually to move, as we contemplate them, in a continuous rhythm.

A two-fold screen by Korin depicts the "Thirty-six Chief Poets of Japan." We look down on a floor simply carpeted with poets. Suppose that you have been presented with thirty-six poets, and asked to arrange them in an agreeable group. How would you compose them? I think your instinct would be to make a central group around a single central figure, ruggedly venerable or radiantly youthful according to your preference, and then to arrange the others symmetrically on either side, disguising the symmetry as artfully as possible. You would have before you the classic example of Raphael and of Ingres.

But Korin does nothing of the kind. There is no centre; there is no symmetry. The composition is all a balance of complex relations. Instead of the light and shade of nature, there is a pattern of light and dark tones. It is a working out of ideas of design, inherited from the older art of Asia but pushed to a point of gay audacity.

Indeed there is at times in Korin's painting a certain arrogance, a touch of bravado, which is foreign to the mood of the greatest art. But he was equally celebrated for his lacquer designs. And in his lacquer-boxes, decorated with lead and mother-of-pearl, Korin seems more controlled, more classic in his style. Lacquer work has been practised from ancient times in Japan, and the Japanese lacquer surpasses that of the Chinese. With their unique patience, thoroughness, and sensitive exactness, the Japanese have produced things of an almost incredible fineness of surface and of workmanship, rivalling the beauty of rare shells. The box reproduced (Pl. 60) is famous. It has grandeur in smallness; a profound sense of style.

Here perhaps we find Japanese art at its most Japanese. But already in this seventeenth century there was forming another school also national in its character. This is the school called Ukiyo-ye, that is, the Painting of the Passing World. It is best known to us through the colour-prints, but though these were all designed by artists of the school, there were many painters who kept to painting only.

In a former lecture I showed you one or two examples of Chinese genre painting, ascribed to masters of the T'ang dynasty. But we have no reason to suppose that there was any direct imitation of Chinese models, or that such models were known to the Japanese.

In Japan, as in Europe, it was long before the painting of the contemporary scene for its own sake was thought worthy of an artist's aim. In mediaeval pictures of the lives of saints there is many a glimpse of what was before the painter's eyes, but such glimpses were merely episodical. In the sixteenth century some painters of the older schools would paint a pleasure-party on a picnic, but furtively and anonymously.

177

Matabei, who was the first to find themes from daily life worthy of serious painting, or at least the first to take such themes exclusively for his province, is a master whose authentic work seems to be very rare, but who inspired a whole group of followers. His example sowed a seed which produced abundant fruit. So we have an array of paintings, screens, and panels, some of which are of great charm. The panel reproduced, one of a pair, with its strong rhythm of dancers in movement, may serve as an example (Pl. 61).

I shall have more to say next week on art in its relation to daily life; for the moment let us note that, though this school is called the Painting of the Passing World, it is very far indeed from the close approach to the life before the painter's eyes that we have become accustomed to in the West. It still keeps much of an abstract form; it portrays the rhythmic movement behind appearances rather than the appearances themselves.

In other schools also "Back to nature!" was the cry. It is the art of these naturalistic schools of the eighteenth and nineteenth centuries with which Japanese painting is associated in the minds of most people in the West. There is perceptible in these schools a new wave of influence from contemporary China, along with a certain influence from Europe. Japan was now once more secluded from the world, cut off from foreign intercourse. Yet through the Dutch, who alone were allowed a very restricted footing in the country, European prints and paintings of some sort filtered in, and were admired by certain Japanese artists. They had the charm no doubt of forbidden fruit.

We saw how in India the painters of the Moghul school were so fascinated by prints brought by the Jesuits that they attempted to imitate the European effects of relief and atmosphere. This did not happen in Japan. Here and there we find an artist who plays with European perspective, as a new game, or introduces cast shadows, just for fun. But the naturalistic schools, though the most prominent of their leaders, Okyo, professed great admiration for Western art, kept to the fundamental Asian conventions. These painters produced a mass of deft and graceful pictures, but they are of little significance in the whole Oriental tradition.

It was natural enough, when the older schools were so manifestly being paralyzed by a dead-alive routine of repetition, that an exhortation to

179

study nature instead of old masters should have been eagerly listened to. But naturalism, exclusively pursued, is a blind alley and always will be.

Let us go back to something which is more expressive of the inner spirit of Japanese art: to the "Waterfall of Nachi," one of the oldest Japanese landscapes which exists (Pl. 62). It was once thought to be by a ninth-century master, Kanaoka, from whom modern scepticism has abstracted all his works. It is no doubt some centuries later. Do we need any more of nature than there is here? And yet how much more it gives us than a reflection of the actual scene! This happened to be the last picture which I saw in Japan, though I had seen it once before. I thought it, I still think it, one of the most beautiful landscapes in the world. It is quite different from any Chinese landscape. A certain purity, a certain severity, in the prolonged lines of the design recall rather the early carved Bodhisattvas with their flowing forms. The sun is just rising above the high crags. Crimson maples appear among the rocks. But it is the silvery, slender fall that holds the eye. The imagined sound of the water falling, as it has been falling for a thousand years, only accentuates the solitude and the stillness.

It was a December afternoon when I took leave of this picture in its owner's house, hanging in the alcove. The brief daylight was going, the early dusk coming on; but I could not help begging Mr. Nezu that the picture might remain, and not be rolled up like the others. I wanted to see the last of it, while any light lingered.

As perhaps you know, the Japanese temples have bells of enormous size which are struck by great suspended beams of wood; and when they are struck, the sound goes out through the pinewoods and into the surrounding air with deeptoned vibrations that only after an incredibly long time are re-absorbed into silence. The effect of these vibrations on the hearer is powerful and strange; it is a kind of disembodying of material things, a momentary initiation into some world beyond range of sight or touch. And contemplating the picture, I felt as if I were listening to those prolonged tones of the evening bell. The waterfall now glimmering in the twilight seemed to be purged of all the accidents of appearance; to be an essence, a spirit, a symbol. I seemed to be in presence of something hidden from the outer world, the continuing soul of a race.

PLATE 46

WOOD KWANNON AT HORYUJI, NARA. JAPAN, SUIKO PERIOD

PLATE 47

WOOD KWANNON AT CHUGUJI NUNNERY, NARA. JAPAN, SUIKO PERIOD

PLATE 48

TACHIBANA BRONZE TRINITY AT HORYUJI, NARA. JAPAN, HAKUHO PERIOD

PLATE 49

YAMAGOSHI AMIDA. JAPAN, SCHOOL OF ESHIN, *ca.* 12TH CENTURY

PLATE 50

PALACE LADIES AND GARDEN, ILLUSTRATING "THE TALE OF GENJI." JAPAN, FUJIWARA PERIOD

PLATE 51

FIGHTING BULLS, FROM A SCROLL BY TOBA SOJO. JAPAN, 12TH CENTURY

PLATE 52

HORSEMAN AMONG PINES, FROM THE SCROLLS OF THE MONGOL INVASION.
JAPAN, KAMAKURA PERIOD

PLATE 53

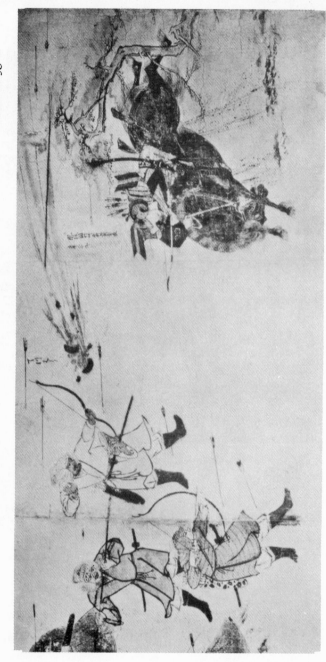

THE REPULSE OF THE MONGOLS, FROM THE SCROLLS OF THE MONGOL INVASION. JAPAN, KAMAKURA PERIOD

PLATE 54

THE SAINT KOBO DAISHI AS A BOY, BY NOBUZANE. JAPAN, 13TH CENTURY

PLATE 55

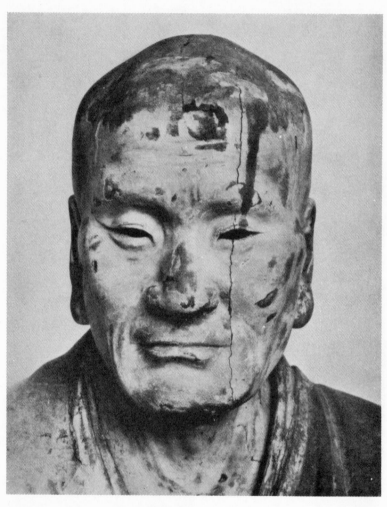

WOODEN STATUE (DETAIL), ATTRIBUTED TO UNKEI. JAPAN, 13TH CENTURY

PLATE 56

INK LANDSCAPE, BY SOAMI.
JAPAN, ASHIKAGA PERIOD

PLATE 57

PINES IN WINTRY HILLS, BY YEITOKU. JAPAN, ASHIKAGA PERIOD

PLATE 58

BROOK IN AUTUMN, BY KOYETSU. JAPAN, 16TH-17TH CENTURY

PLATE 59

MOONRISE, ATTRIBUTED TO SOTATSU. JAPAN, 17TH CENTURY

PLATE 60

LACQUER BOX, TORII AND FAGOT FENCE, BY KORIN. JAPAN, TOKUGAWA PERIOD

PLATE 61

DANCERS. JAPAN, MATABEI SCHOOL,
TOKUGAWA PERIOD

PLATE 62

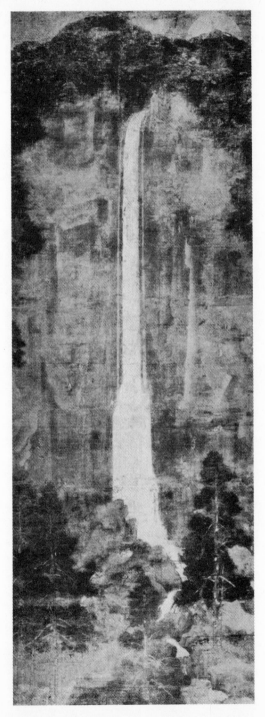

WATERFALL OF NACHI, ATTRIBUTED TO KANAOKA.
JAPAN, FUJIWARA PERIOD

Lecture VI

I HAVE tried to show how in the creative art of Asia the spirit of man has expressed itself not less richly and abundantly than in the art of the West, and at the same time how surely, even in this art which is strange to most of us, one can gauge the degree of sensibility, the quality of emotion and understanding, the depth of imagination, whatever be the work presented to our eyes.

We have roamed over this great continent, alighting here and there to contemplate certain aspects of its art in certain periods. I have shown you glimpses only, but enough, I hope, to exhibit the interwoven threads that knit the arts of these countries together; and, more than that, to illustrate the real solidarity of mankind. We have of course had to leave whole tracts unvisited and unexplored. I have said nothing, for instance, of Cambodia or of Indonesia; of the Buddhist sculptures in high relief, so full of varied grace and animation, at Borobudur in Java; of the marvellous friezes and statues adorning the fabulous temples of Angkor.

You may perhaps think that in attempting to appraise the special excellences of Eastern art I have depreciated by implication the art of the West. Such was not my purpose. I cannot myself understand how if one appreciates the masterpieces of the one continent one can fail to appreciate the masterpieces of the other. When we descend to lower levels it is no doubt different. Western art degenerates into literalism and a slavery to fact and appearance; Eastern art degenerates into fanciful arabesque. There we can exercise and enjoy our natural dislikes. What I have had in mind is the necessity, in approaching an art which is new to us in its conventions and subject-matter, of getting rid of prejudices and prepossessions, both our own and other people's. I think of those lines in Wordsworth's "Poet's Epitaph":

> And you must love him, ere to you
> He will seem worthy of your love.

That is true of works of art no less than of human beings. Criticism from the outside is of little value to anyone.

How great an obstacle those prejudices and prepossessions can be, if we acquiesce in them, is manifest from the story of the gradual revelation of Oriental art to Europe. May I remind

you of the way and the order in which this discovery was made?

The man who might have told us something
of the glories of Chinese art at its greatest,
Marco Polo, mentions in his account of Hang-
chow some paintings in palaces of fair ladies and
warriors and wonderful histories. But it is evi-
dent that he cast on them but a casual eye; he
was vastly more impressed with the outward
amenities of the city, the three hundred hot-
water baths, the markets, the police, the courtesy of the inhabitants, the throng of fashionable
carriages on the road by the lake, the profusion of
palaces and temples. What to the Chinese were
the things of the spirit were to him but futile
superstitions, the fancies of the idolaters; only
things to be despised. This was the general
attitude of Western travellers in Asia. The
Western conviction of superiority, and obstinate
determination to impose external standards,
prevented any serious approach to Eastern art
till late in the nineteenth century.

Before that we have sporadic examples of
Oriental influence in the West. It was possible
to appreciate Persian carpets, Chinese porcelain, Japanese lacquer, without the prejudices
aroused by an alien world of thought and an

alien method of representation. But they were
regarded as the work of highly gifted artisans:
the fine arts, as we call them, were the preroga-
tive of Europe. Rembrandt made free copies
from the miniatures in an album of paintings of
the Moghul school; Archbishop Laud possessed
a book of Hindu drawings as early as 1640. But
the appeal was mainly to curiosity. The
"curio," which one could admire with a certain
agreeable condescension, is still for most people
the type of Eastern art.

In the seventeenth and eighteenth centuries
there was indeed a great wave of Chinese influence on the arts of decoration. Porcelain,
wall-papers, figured silks, lacquer, furniture,
were largely imported. *Chinoiseries* became the
fashion. Watteau and his followers found
happy hints and motives in the playful fantasies
of Chinese designers. They inspired Chippen-
dale to new forms of chairs and cabinets. The
porcelain factories of Europe vied with each
other in imitating wares of China. It was never
realized that the designs on porcelains merely
reflected the Chinese painting of the day.

But I imagine that the most fruitful seeds of
influence were sown by the designs of wall-
papers and silks.

The mediaeval artists of Europe, the carvers in wood and stone, the illuminators of manuscripts, had shown a natural delight in the beauty of wild flowers, the shapes of leaves, the life of the birds among the leaves. They could not portray sacred scenes or persons without their fancy overflowing at the same time into flower and tendril. But with the Renaissance decoration returned to geometry. The Greeks, it appeared, had in all nature noticed one plant only: the acanthus. The Greeks must be followed. And when the wealth of nature and the floral world were rediscovered by the designers of interior decoration, it was the Chinese designs, I think, which showed the way, rather than a revival of mediaeval traditions. I spoke in a former lecture of the world of animal life intermediate between mankind and the mysteries of the outer and unexplained world beyond, peopled with vague terrors; and I might have dwelt not only on the life of animals, but on the life of flowers, both so little regarded for their own sake in Europe during the centuries when the Renaissance obsession with human personality and its pride of power dominated the themes of art. It was not only the discovery of a wealth of pictorial motives in the

187

world of flowers which drew on the Chinese, it was a different conception of the universe. They have always associated flowers with birds; as if the songs from the birds' throats, as they flit among the foliage and leave the boughs trembling, made articulate the flowers' silent joy in their expansion and reaching up toward the light. So the human spirit is led on from one relationship to another, in the complex web of life.

About 1860 some stray Japanese colourprints found their way to Europe. (Specimens came to Holland in the late eighteenth and early nineteenth centuries, but they seem mostly to have disappeared; at any rate, they caused no excitement.) The first prints which arrived in Paris are said to have been used as wrappings for articles of commerce; for these prints were cheap things in Japan, not highly prized at all. Some artists seized on them with cries of joy. More prints were sent for; collectors contended for them. We all know how much they meant to the art of Degas and of Whistler. They also transformed the whole art of the poster. They showed how telling economy of line and colour could be. It was the Japanese prints which first made people in the West surmise that Asian art might be something more than exquisite

188

handicraft and the adornment of things of use. It was supposed at first that the prints represented the culmination of the pictorial art of Japan; and Japanese art was assumed to be the one Oriental art capable of comparison with the art of the West. Edmond de Goncourt pronounced that Hokusai and Utamaro were the greatest of Japanese masters.

America was more fortunate. A few men of enlightenment, especially Fenollosa, seized the truth that the really great art of Japan was the art of far earlier periods, and that the still greater art of China lay behind that. Nor must we forget in England William Anderson, whose collection of Japanese and Chinese paintings was bought by the British Museum in 1880, and who certainly discerned things in their true perspective.

In fifty years how much has been discovered! Japanese publications with their marvellous reproductions opened up to us all the classics of Japanese painting and sculpture, and the splendid examples of Chinese art preserved in Japan. Collectors began to turn to China. Chinese paintings began to be imported into Europe and America. Archaeologists of many countries were sent to China and Chinese

Turkestan; and all the wealth of Chinese Buddhist sculpture, still surviving in spite of the vast
amount of destruction that has been wrought,
was revealed.

The Buddhist art of China inevitably led to
the Buddhist art of India, and so to Indian art
in general. For though Indian sculpture and
architecture had been known to Europeans for
some centuries, Indian art had been regarded
merely as "heathen idols," the hideous study of
the ethnologist. It is only in this century, too,
and in quite recent years, that Persian art has
begun, or rather is beginning, to receive anything like its due, Persian painting in particular.
Thus it was the art of the Farthest East that first
opened the eyes of the West, and the art of the
Nearer East that is the last to be appreciated.

What had happened to change the Western
attitude? It was not only the discoveries themselves, it was something that had overtaken
Western art.

As a broad generalization, I think it is true
that in Europe since the Renaissance the zest
of exploration, the absorption of new material,
the adoption of new methods of expression, have
been the most stimulating incentives to creative
artists. The scientific element inevitably plays

190

an important part in all mature painting; but in Europe this element had been cultivated to excess. Correct anatomy, correct perspective, representation of light and shade and of atmospheric effect — these were supposed to be essential things in pictorial art. But when all these had been mastered, so that the visual impression of a scene could be thrown in its completeness on to a canvas, there was a sudden stop. What remained to be done along these lines? Nothing. A recoil was inevitable. It was perceived that these scientific elements, important as they were, were a means and not an end. We were thrown back from the painting of appearances to something really fundamental: rhythmical design. And so it became much more easy to appreciate art which used a different mode of representation.

It is not unnatural perhaps that now, when we have some idea of the range of Asian art, and the heights of which it is capable, many people should despise the Japanese colourprints as pretty toys and no more.

But let us take them for what they are. They do not pretend to be anything but a popular art. And where else has the passing scene of daily life inspired an art comparable to this in richness and variety, as in sheer distinction of colour and design?

In Asia, the only sort of parallel that occurs to me is the drawings and small paintings of the Rajput school in India. I showed you one of these the other day, as a specimen of line-drawing, and compared it with a Persian line-drawing. But it serves also to illustrate the popular art of India. This school is popular in the sense that it is not mainly concerned, like the Moghul school, with the glorification of kings and nobles, the portraiture of their persons and the depicting of their sports. It is concerned mainly with everyday life, and with popular legends, especially the legends of Krishna, the Divine Cowherd.

One favourite set of themes is the Ragmalas and Raginis, as they are called. These are musical motives, associated with the seasons, the times of the day, and also with certain moods and occasions. The pictorial counterparts to those musical themes have a peculiar charm, being full of a natural poetry.

Most of these paintings and line-drawings date from the eighteenth and nineteenth centuries. The woman waiting for her lover at night under a blossoming tree, while the shy deer

come to peep at her (Pl. 63), is the counterpart
of one of these musical modes and the theme of
many a lovely painting.

It may be that the woman is Radha waiting
for her divine lover Krishna. We meet again
the mystic feeling, easily misunderstood, which
we met in Persian art, in the numberless drawings of Krishna's sport and dalliance with his
playmates, the milkmaids. One of the finest
paintings of Krishna themes is the "Cowdust"
— the returning of Krishna with the herd
at evening to the city — in the Boston
Museum.

These drawings were usually intended to be
coloured, but were often left uncoloured; and
in such cases we enjoy all the more the delicacy
and sureness of the line. The fluid lines seem
to jet like water from a fountain curving over
as it falls. Such line-drawing affects one like
overhearing a young voice singing for pleasure.
Since art is sensuous, since all it has to convey
must be communicated through the senses, the
medium of communication is of the first importance. And in the best of these drawings the
mood is communicated with no impediment in
the utterance, with perfect felicity. In the
British Museum is an example of a painting

193

partly coloured and left unfinished. It is the bride who has just bidden farewell to the two chosen friends of her girlhood. The light colouring is like that of some early Italian fresco. The combined tenderness and reticence remind one of scenes in classic Indian drama, like *Sakuntala*, with their sweet and normal human feeling. Conceived in a slightly different mood is a toilet scene (Pl. 64) designed in a roundel. There is an atmosphere as of ritual ceremony, and the two girls who incline their heads above the screening curtain have the air of heads in some romantic early drawing by Rossetti.

This art of the Kangra valley has the same sort of fresh charm as — if one may compare one art with another — the lyrics of the Elizabethan songbooks. In both cases there is continual variation on a few chosen themes. The desire to be original, to break fresh ground, is absent. It is the familiar that is expected, and the variation is what wins the audience. Tradition is not departed from. Such an art as this exhausts itself before long. The sweetness is apt to become over-sweet, and cloy. But there is virility as well as grace in the drawing of a young warrior (Pl. 65), reminding us in its purity of line of the drawing on a Greek pot.

You may say that these drawings, at least those which take their themes from the legends of Krishna and Rama and Siva and Parvati, should be classed with religious art. But religion is so much a part of daily existence in India that they have a truly popular character, especially when we contrast them with the paintings of the Moghul school. Nevertheless the world they represent is small and circumscribed compared with the world of the Japanese woodcuts.

For surely there is no popular art in the world to compare with these colour-prints. They were produced, remember, solely by artisans and small shopkeepers, for people of that class. Kiyonaga, a master of stately design, retired in middle life to become a tobacconist.

It is true that the conditions in which this art flourished were peculiar and, in a sense, artificial. Japan from the opening of the seventeenth century had been once more closed to the outer world. The feudal system was a rigid order; and within this strict frame the various classes of the population had each a separate existence. If a Samurai deigned to go to the popular theatre, with which the colour-prints were so closely connected, he would go in disguise. The aristocratic connoisseur and collector would disdain these cheap sheets because of the vulgar associations, as he would consider them, of their subject-matter. That prejudice still lingers in Japan.

Possibly the water-colours of Rowlandson form the nearest analogue, with their vivid and gay picture of life, their happy rhythm of line and charm of colour. But then Rowlandson, though he produced thousands of drawings, was a single artist; whereas Ukiyo-ye, the school which produced the colour prints, could number hundreds of artists, some of them very highly gifted. Then, too, it was not so much the drawings by Rowlandson which were popular, as the prints which he etched and which were coloured by hand. And the subjects he chose to etch were mostly satirical or amusing in a rather gross fashion, things to raise a laugh, or invoke the spirit of mockery.

Would you not expect that an art produced for the entertainment of such people as I have described would attempt a similar appeal? would find butts for its ridicule, objects for its derision? But satire is rare. A few satirical prints were published at one time or another, but were promptly pounced upon by the Government, and the designers punished. There is fun sometimes; but even fun is rather rare. There is often a playful thought behind the design, but this hardly appears on the surface. No, it is rather a sweet seriousness which pervades these prints.

It is hard for us to realize, especially in the present day, what it is to be self-enclosed as a nation, to have no dealings with the world outside and no news of it. But even within Japan there were in the eighteenth century no politics, no elections, no newspapers, no magnates contending for popular applause and support.

The people were thrown back on themselves and their own resources. They were, I imagine, poor and hard-working; yet from the evidence of the prints one would say that they enjoyed a good deal of leisure. The prints reflect chiefly the amusements of the people.

The employment of leisure is with us today a problem that causes a certain disquietude and threatens to cause more in the future. Machines are to give us all increasing spare time; and how are we to employ it? Even allowing for the natural tendency to sentimentalize a past age, we must admit that these Japanese artisans could read us a lesson in "the art of living in the world."

What sources did they draw on for their pleasure?

Consider for a moment the motives of decoration used in the patterns of the dresses. The Japanese taste is sober; it does not delight in exuberance of colour so much as in subtle harmonies of colour. But if we look through any series of Japanese prints with an eye to the patterns, we find a richness of invention that is quite unparalleled elsewhere, even in China.

There are simple and primary elements such as are familiar also to us — spots, stripes, chequers, lozenges; but these forms are used with, and foiled by, motives drawn from the whole world of nature. Flowers of course are there, flowers of all seasons: the plum-blossom, the cherry, the iris, the chrysanthemum; the snow-covered leaves of the bamboo; red maple leaves; uncurling fern-fronds. Intermingled with these are motives like the flight of the wild geese, or the spray-like flight of small plovers over breaking waves; then there will be the sea-waves themselves; sails upon the sea; petals adrift on streams; shells on the seashore; the fantastic pattern of cracks in ice; horses in the meadows; the trailing boughs of willows; carp leaping up torrents; dragons; showers of fans;

showers of love-letters — there is absolutely no end to these themes of decoration. The patterns are not formally repeating patterns, as with us. And since the whole conception of design in Japan is so far removed from realism, there is no incongruous naturalism. It is the same with the objects and utensils used in daily life. Perhaps nowhere else in the world has the sense of beauty been so pervasive.

The point about the decorative motives in the colour-prints is this. The artists were not simply aiming to make a blank space interesting and agreeable; it was their instinct rather to weave into their daily lives reminders and suggestions of all that most delighted and entertained them in the lovely world without.

All through Japanese life runs a vein of what one might call a courtesy to nature; as if it was felt that to pass by any manifestation of beauty in nature was like neglecting a courtesy to a human being. True to the Asian tradition which we found in China many centuries before, these artists, these people, are imbued with a sense of companionship with all that lives. This makes for happiness. It opens up springs of pleasure on every side, not exciting enough perhaps for our own public, which would probably consider the holiday occupations of these Japanese youths and girls, such as writing poems in April and hanging them on the blossoming boughs, a great waste of time.

This world of Ukiyo-ye is limited, but remarkable for its completeness. In the space of a century and a half it mirrors the life of the people, or rather this particular section of the people, with endless variety, and then it goes on to picture the setting of that life, and even its roots in the past. At first sight the school appears to be self-enclosed. The creation of a populace, and existing only for their taste and pleasure, it seems to be cut off from the world of thought, philosophy, scholarship, religion, in which the older art is steeped. But as we look closer, we find how lightly and spontaneously it attaches itself to all the national inheritance of the mind. This does not appear on the surface. We seem to be looking merely at a scene from daily life, but again and again we discover that the scene is so conceived as to carry an allusion to an old classic poem, to a Chinese or Indian legend. This is what is so amazing in this popular art, and still more in the public to which it appealed, the awareness of all that complex mental tradition having its far-off roots in the history of the Asian continent.

These artists will often take a subject from one of the old schools of painting, and substitute for sage or saint the figure of a girl dressed in the fashion of the day; whether just in playfulness or as if with a sort of challenging question, "Isn't she much more attractive than your old sages and saints?" — who shall say? Harunobu sets one of his small slender figures on the wings of a flying stork, instead of the Taoist hermit who was wont to fly thus through the air. And in another print it is a girl who plays the part of Daruma, the grim patriarch of the Zen sect, crossing the ocean on a reed.

When we look at his print of a woman leading a child and with a bucket of water on her head, we take it for what it is, an incident from life, a charming design; but the motive of it is the parallel of a moment in the life of the servant-girl, weary of her lot, to a moment in the life of a famous poetess of the ninth century, who in her youth was wooed by many lovers for her beauty and wit, but in her old age became a miserable wanderer and cried out in a poem her longing to be released from her identity and to die.

Again, in an early morning interior we see a

girl looking at the mouse which the boy has caught; but the real motive is the shadow of the pine-tree. "I have dusted the paper-shutter clean of every speck: how beautiful the image of the pine-tree!" The little poem suggests the sweeping of the mind to receive the image of beauty.

This is something different from burlesque or parody. The spirit is different. It is not so much a bringing down of the classic poetry to the level of common life as an affirmation that common life is worthy of poetry, no less than the life of the gorgeous grandees and ladies of the Middle Ages.

Harunobu indeed depends on no inspiration from outside. He is a natural poet. Suddenly in 1764 the colour-print in many colours — preceded by a long period during which the woodcuts were coloured by hand or printed in two colours only, red and green — the full colour-print was invented, and at the same time the genius of this artist expanded like a tree that has burst into blossom overnight. The world he paints is all springtime, all youth. The girl lingering on the verandah, oblivious for the moment of her lover's hand pulling at her because of the poignant beauty of the blossom illuminated in the beam of her lantern, typifies Harunobu's art. Youth or spring: which is lovelier? (Pl. 66.)

I suggested last week that the exclusive pursuit of a certain aim was a Japanese characteristic. And Harunobu seems to say: "Youth and bloom — what else is worth depicting, when these are so magical, so intoxicating?" He pours out print after print, exquisite in colour, as if afraid that life will not leave him time to explore all the riches of his theme. In fact before six years were over he was dead. You might think that so exclusive a dwelling on "favour and prettiness" would lead to an insipid sweetness. But there is always a certain squareness of design, however delicate and flowerlike the types. It is not a question of pretty faces only, as it was apt to be in eighteenth-century Europe,

In daily life, if we watch people doing something intently (and the whole body will be occupied when the mind is absorbed in an action) — it may be merely a girl threading a needle, a child playing with a toy, a carpenter planing wood — they spontaneously fascinate our attention, they seem to draw us into their own lives, or rather into some impersonal energy, into life itself.

The charm of this art of the colour-print lies in its discovery of the inexhaustible beauty that there is in the natural, one might say "animal," movements and attitudes of the human body, and the natural relationship of these forms to other forms. The turn of a head, the clasp of a hand, the stooping to tie a sandal that has become undone, any such simple movement — how beautiful it can be when it is unself-conscious! Our pictorial art is full of figures which want to call the spectator's attention to themselves, or which are indulging in movements and gestures dictated only by the requirements of composition. It is rare to find figures like those of Rembrandt, each absolutely absorbed in what he or she is doing, and totally unconscious of a spectator. None of the Japanese print-designers has a mind like Rembrandt's with its profound and wide humanity. But they have this rare merit, at least the masters among them, of seeing the living form as it is, undiverted from its natural ways and functions. They are single-minded in their aim of presenting the transient scene of daily life in its own beauty. They feel that this life, too, has its inherent dignity.

In Utamaro this recognition is accompanied by a rare gift of invention in design. His theme is Woman. More and more the theme engrosses him, as Youth had engrossed Harunobu. Often he draws woman at the mirror, that little world which encloses the treasure of her beauty. What force is given to the design (Pl. 67) by the swing of the figures, accentuating the almost fierce intentness of the girl combing back her hair, and how admirably the two forms are brought into relation!

With the same intentness Utamaro studies woman in every phase of her existence. He is interested in feminine character. He paints various types of feminine physiognomy. But, as the years go on, it is woman as mother that engrosses him the most. The ways of a mother with her baby are an inexhaustible source of happy and original design. Sometimes it is a playful incident, as when the mother sleeps and the darling child takes the opportunity to empty out the goldfish bowl; or it is the seizure of a charming moment, as when the young mother with her baby on her shoulder bends down to look at the reflection of their two faces in the well.

By degrees, as if he would probe this maternal emotion to the depths, Utamaro sees it more and more in its primitive, even animal, aspect — a

205

jealous, all-absorbing passion. And for a time he will desert the Transient World and delight in picturing the legend of Kintoki, the strong boy, the infant Hercules of Japan, with his wild foster-mother of the mountains, Yamauba. In such a print as the famous "Yamauba with the Chestnut," he seems to be transcending the limits of the school and its contentment with the daily scene, to pass into a wilder and more elemental region (Pl. 68).

That sense of the primitive is present in this artist's most famous print, the triptych of "Divers for Awabi Shellfish." Again we see a mother and child, the mother combing her wet hair, and behind the group are the waves of the sea, melting into haze.

In another artist, the most varied, prolific, and powerful of the school, Hokusai, we discover a similar impulse to burst the bonds of its tradition and escape into a larger world. Hokusai, greatly ambitious, studied all the masters in turn, Chinese as well as Japanese; and when at the age of sixty he struck his most original vein it was in emulation of the Chinese masters that he produced his great landscape-prints. But instead of monochrome he used full colour in frank opposition, but so boldly simplified as not to impair the unity and largeness of the design. Fuji towers red against a blue morning barred with white cloud. The "Deep-sea Wave" with its toppling crest owes its haunting power less to observation than to imaginative vision.

What part had such themes in the Passing World? These were the everlasting things of nature. Yet after all they were the background of the transient life of men and women; and they belonged to Japan. The people, led by the artists, began to be conscious of the beauties of their own land. How could they have been content so long with the endless pictures of an imaginary China? how neglected so long the ravishing aspects of the hills and bays, the pine-forests and sea-shores?

Again one marvels at this public, to whom Hokusai's so personal interpretations of nature, with their dramatic and sometimes bizarre contrasts of colour, could be acceptable.

With Hiroshige, Hokusai's later contemporary, it is different. We can understand how everyone could appreciate his intimate feeling for the Japanese country, his extraordinary fidelity to its atmosphere. Travelling the great highroads by the coast and the mountains, he designed countless prints. And he gave, what none of the older painters had given, the colour of Japan, the beauty of the rain, of the snow, of the twilight, of the starry darkness. With him all is redolent of the soil responsive to every subtle variation of the weather. His prints are as true to Japanese country as Constable's canvases — they were actually contemporaries — to English country.

Then, to complete the achievement of the school, in the mid-nineteenth century another artist, Kuniyoshi, appeals to another side of the awakening of the people. The school had first held up a mirror to the life of every day; then with the landscape-prints it had disclosed the charm of the country to which the people belonged. In both cases the appeal was to what was before their eyes. But now, in print after print depicting heroic episodes in the past history of Japan, it appealed to the consciousness of the race, to its memory and pride. It was all part of that stirring and expansion which led in 1868 to the restoration of the Emperor. This reawakening would hardly have been possible without the popular theatre, which made the heroic past familiar to the people. And the innumerable colour-prints of actors and scenes in plays made it doubly familiar.

Kuniyoshi's subjects are frequently taken from episodes of the civil wars, the themes of the thirteenth-century masters who painted on long rolls the battles of that time. They are dramatic, perhaps rather melodramatic. I prefer to show you a print (Pl. 69) of an episode in the life of that stormy spirit the saint Nichiren of the thirteenth century, where, exiled to a lonely island, he makes his way painfully from the shore up the snow-covered hillside.

In a sense this is a highly abstract art. There is no imitation of surface-textures; there are no shadows, no effects of light and shade. And yet in an art avowedly devoted to portraying the transient world these things are what we should expect the artists of such a school to be occupied upon.

I think one might compare the conventions of the Japanese print-designers to the use of verse in drama. The verse keeps the dialogue at a certain remove from actuality while stressing the rhythm of speech. So the print-designers by removing from the given scene all the accidents of appearance, the play of light and shade, give it a certain ideality; and at the same time their instinct leads them to stress the rhythmical element in their designs.

One must admire the public which bought these prints as much as the artists who produced them. This public is not delighted by the kind of drawing which makes one exclaim "How like!" The feminine figures, for instance, are types rather than individuals; and they change from infantine and delicate to tall and majestic proportions, and then back again, with very little reference to the actual Japanese type of figure.

When these prints were first disclosed to Europe, there were those who hailed them as pure art — design in line and colour, and nothing more. They found they could appreciate them without knowing anything of their content, associations, or background; therefore, they concluded, content and background didn't matter in art.

They wanted to abstract the form from the content. I submit that this cannot be done.

Look at this Chinese vase (Pl. 70), made more than a thousand years ago. Out of mere clay, out of the element of the earth itself, human hands have wrought this shape. Mind and matter meet in it; and the rude matter has been related to human desires and feelings, so that here you might say that matter is spiritualized.

There is no conscious attempt to express anything; but the curves of the shape do express energy and control, they have the full contour of a ripe fruit, not the nerveless and unnourished lines of feeble animation; and the very texture of the material has become eloquent to the touch. No less than a great picture or statue, this vase typifies what art is and what art does: how it has its being in the world of the senses yet communicates through the senses so much more than we can express in words. You cannot tell the body from the spirit, the thing expressed from its expression. The complete work is filled with a mysterious life like a human personality.

In a successful work of mature art, however complex, there is the same integrity. There is a fusion of all the elements that make up the whole. But a plausible attempt can be made to separate the elements.

The moralist, a Tolstoi for instance, perceives the power that art exerts and looks at it as an electrician looks at running water; he wants to harness it for social use. He wants to tear from the work of art a meaning helpful to people in their conduct toward each other.

The aesthete, on the other hand, wants to detach the form from the matter, and claims that we should value the work solely for its appeal to the aesthetic sense, said to be concerned solely with relations between forms, masses, spaces, and so on.

In either case impoverishment results.

Theories apart, however, these prints, and still more the whole art of Asia as it was gradually disclosed, taught us a much-needed lesson. They reminded us of the true language of art. They reminded us that this language is not addressed to the mere intelligence, at any rate not directly. Its appeal is far deeper.

Pictorial design uses a language which speaks to something in our inner nature beyond the reach of words.

Design is founded on the simple elements of straight line and curve. And what is more expressive than those primary elements? Order and liberty, reason and imagination, control and energy — these antagonized yet inseparable principles are combined in every human conception of a life worth living. The image of that contrast and combination is expressed in the fluid, flexible lines of nature contrasted and combined with the straight lines and angles of man's ruling. And according as one element or the other predominates, there are produced types of design, types of decoration, which affect us in very different ways.

Straight line and curve, repetition and contrast — these are the foundation. But growing up out of these is the whole marvellous structure of pictorial design, in which other elements gradually play their part: the potency of space, reserves, and silences; the potency of light and dark, the eloquence of tone; the potency of imagined mass and volume; the glory and vibration of the lyric notes of colour.

That is the language of pictorial art. And how many European painters have thrown these rich resources away, trying to let form and colour do the work of words instead of letting them speak for themselves!

Yet this language, no less than verbal language when used in poetry, communicates a meaning, a significance. Even when used just for the joy of its use, it cannot help communicating something. What is that something?

Art has no existence apart from the bodily senses. And yet it is a spiritual activity. It is concerned solely with appearances, yet in its own way, no less than Philosophy or Science, it seeks for and discovers something behind appearances.

What is this quest? Not intangible, abstract ideas, the quest of Philosophy. Not invisible elements and energies, the quest of Science. What then? It is something real, something that profoundly satisfies the whole man — not his intellect only, or his emotions only, or his senses only. If one must suggest a name, I can only suggest Life itself. Not life as we know it in our thwarted, care-burdened, precarious existence, but life as we desire it to be, and as we experience it in moments when simply to be alive seems something more precious than any possession.

When a young man talks of "seeing life," and when we read in the New Testament of "having life more abundantly," the same word is used but with a different meaning. In one case it is the life of the senses, in the other the life of the spirit. Yet where is the dividing line? You cannot separate the spirit from the body. Art is a perpetual witness to that. It is the meeting place of spirit and sense, which so many have tried to set in opposition and divorce from one another.

Life delights in life. Surely that is what lies behind the imitative instinct, so manifest in mankind. Next to the enjoyment of our own bodily activity is the enjoyment of watching other living creatures in movement.

That would seem to have been the original impulse of Palaeolithic Man, the impulse which set him to capture life in the forms of the animals he traced on the walls of his cave. The Neolithic Man represents the other type of artist, the born decorator. To trace running lines and curves on clay or metal, and then relate them to each other, was to him a kind of overflow, like a breaking into song or moving the limbs to music in the dance. In the one there is a flowing out, in the other a drawing in. In perfected art these two types, the representative and the rhythmic, coalesce.

But this is not quite all.

In a former lecture I alluded to that instinct or desire in man which impels him to pass out of his own being, to become different from what he is. The art of the drama exemplifies in a special way this instinct: there is a desire to assume other personalities and explore them. But I wonder if in other arts this desire, or something like it, be not present. For the draughtsman, if he is to make a drawing that has life, must in a sense become what he draws. He must feel in himself the tensions and impulses that control the movements of the body before him; he must feel the growing of the tree, the weight and mass of the rock.

Just as there is a continuity in life throughout the universe from the plant and the mollusc to the highest reach of human power, to the hero, the saint, and the sage, to the man who will gladly sacrifice his own life to preserve the life of his ideal, so there is a continuity in art. It rises on the one hand from the vivid sketch with little or no design, on the other from the pattern on dish or basket which is design and nothing else, to the supreme masterpiece which is inexhaustible in its fullness and mystery, and rejoices generation after generation.

If there is one thing more than another that we can learn from Eastern art it is this continuity. There we find no sterilizing divorce between "fine" art and "decorative" art; all art is one.

But though a great Persian carpet may seem for a moment more glorious than any picture ever painted, yet human experience tells us that the most precious and enduring art is not what some would call the purest, but the art which embodies most fully the desires, the exultations, and the agonies of the spirit of man.

I ask your pardon. I had not intended to launch out so far in speculation, probably beyond my depth. Yet I feel that precisely because all this art of Asia has now swum into our ken, and because we are compelled to reconsider the traditional values of the West, it does behove us all to try to clear our minds, and attempt at least to discover what art means to ourselves.

Will anyone ever produce a universally accepted definition of art? I hope not. For what would the aesthetic philosophers do, their occupation gone? Meanwhile we ordinary mortals are free to enjoy the experience of art, each in his own way. It is all, as William Blake called it, "a means of conversing with Paradise."

PLATE 63

TRYST. INDIA, RAJPUT, PAHARI, 18TH CENTURY

PLATE 64

RADHA'S TOILET.
INDIA, RAJPUT, PAHARI, 18TH CENTURY

PLATE 65

YOUNG WARRIOR.
INDIA, RAJPUT, PAHARI, 18TH CENTURY

PLATE 66

LEAVE TAKING AT NIGHT. JAPANESE COLOUR–PRINT BY HARUNOBU

PLATE 67

WOMAN AT MIRROR.
JAPANESE COLOUR–PRINT BY UTAMARO

PLATE 68

YAMAUBA WITH THE CHESTNUT.
JAPANESE COLOUR-PRINT BY UTAMARO

PLATE 69

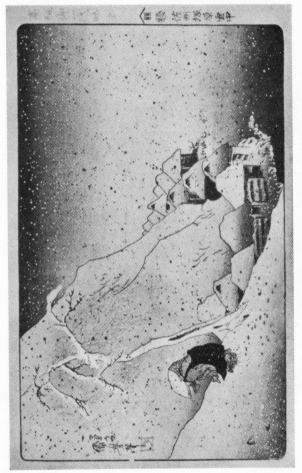

NICHIREN IN EXILE. JAPANESE COLOUR-PRINT BY KUNIYOSHI

PLATE 70

LARGE POTTERY JAR.   CHINA, T'ANG DYNASTY

Dover Books on Art

Dover Books on Art

PRINCIPLES OF ART HISTORY, H. Wölfflin. This remarkably instructive work demonstrates the tremendous change in artistic conception from the 14th to the 18th centuries, by analyzing 164 works by Botticelli, Dürer, Hobbema, Holbein, Hals, Titian, Rembrandt, Vermeer, etc., and pointing out exactly what is meant by "baroque," "classic," "primitive," "picturesque," and other basic terms of art history and criticism. "A remarkable lesson in the art of seeing," SAT. REV. OF LITERATURE. Translated from the 7th German edition. 150 illus. 254pp. 6⅛ x 9¼.   20276-3 Paperbound $2.50

FOUNDATIONS OF MODERN ART, A. Ozenfant. Stimulating discussion of human creativity from paleolithic cave painting to modern painting, architecture, decorative arts. Fully illustrated with works of Gris, Lipchitz, Léger, Picasso, primitive, modern artifacts, architecture, industrial art, much more. 226 illustrations. 368pp. 6⅛ x 9¼.   20215-1 Paperbound $3.00

METALWORK AND ENAMELLING, H. Maryon. Probably the best book ever written on the subject. Tells everything necessary for the home manufacture of jewelry, rings, ear pendants, bowls, etc. Covers materials, tools, soldering, filigree, setting stones, raising patterns, repoussé work, damascening, niello, cloisonné, polishing, assaying, casting, and dozens of other techniques. The best substitute for apprenticeship to a master metalworker. 363 photos and figures. 374pp. 5½ x 8½.

22702-2 Paperbound $3.50

SHAKER FURNITURE, E. D. and F. Andrews. The most illuminating study of Shaker furniture ever written. Covers chronology, craftsmanship, houses, shops, etc. Includes over 200 photographs of chairs, tables, clocks, beds, benches, etc. "Mr. & Mrs. Andrews know all there is to know about Shaker furniture," Mark Van Doren, NATION. 48 full-page plates. 192pp. 7⅞ x 10¾.   20679-3 Paperbound $2.75

ANIMAL DRAWING: ANATOMY AND ACTION FOR ARTISTS, C. R. Knight. 158 studies, with full accompanying text, of such animals as the gorilla, bear, bison, dromedary, camel, vulture, pelican, iguana, shark, etc., by one of the greatest modern masters of animal drawing. Innumerable tips on how to get life expression into your work. "An excellent reference work," SAN FRANCISCO CHRONICLE. 158 illustrations. 156pp. 10½ x 8½.   20426-X Paperbound $3.00

Dover Books on Art

THE COMPLETE BOOK OF SILK SCREEN PRINTING PRO-DUCTION, J. I. Biegeleisen. Here is a clear and complete picture of every aspect of silk screen technique and press operation—from individually operated manual presses to modern automatic ones. Unsurpassed as a guidebook for setting up shop, making shop operation more efficient, finding out about latest methods and equipment; or as a textbook for use in teaching, studying, or learning all aspects of the profession. 124 figures. Index. Bibliography. List of Supply Sources. xi + 253pp. 5⅜ x 8½.

21100-2 Paperbound $2.75

A HISTORY OF COSTUME, Carl Köhler. The most reliable and authentic account of the development of dress from ancient times through the 19th century. Based on actual pieces of clothing that have survived, using paintihgs, statues and other reproductions only where originals no longer exist. Hundreds of illustrations, including detailed patterns for many articles. Highly useful for theatre and movie directors, fashion designers, illustrators, teachers. Edited and augmented by Emma von Sichart. Translated by Alexander K. Dallas. 594 illustrations. 464pp. 5⅛ x 7⅛.

21030-8 Paperbound $3.00

CHINESE HOUSEHOLD FURNITURE, G. N. Kates. A summary of virtually everything that is known about authentic Chinese furniture before it was contaminated by the influence of the West. The text covers history of styles, materials used, principles of design and craftsmanship, and furniture arrangement—all fully illustrated. xiii + 190pp. 5⅝ x 8½.

20958-X Paperbound $1.75

THE COMPLETE WOODCUTS OF ALBRECHT DURER, edited by Dr. Willi Kurth. Albrecht Dürer was a master in various media, but it was in woodcut design that his creative genius reached its highest expression. Here are all of his extant woodcuts, a collection of over 300 great works, many of which are not available elsewhere. An indispensable work for the art historian and critic and all art lovers. 346 plates. Index. 285pp. 8½ x 12¼.

21097-9 Paperbound $3.00

Dover publishes books on commercial art, art history, crafts, design, art classics; also books on music, literature, science, mathematics, puzzles and entertainments, chess, engineering, biology, philosophy, psychology, languages, history, and other fields. For free circulars write to Dept. DA, Dover Publications, Inc., 180 Varick St., New York, N.Y. 10014.

Dover Books on Art

PRINCIPLES OF ART HISTORY, H. Wölfflin. This remarkably instructive work demonstrates the tremendous change in artistic conception from the 14th to the 18th centuries, by analyzing 164 works by Botticelli, Dürer, Hobbema, Holbein, Hals, Titian, Rembrandt, Vermeer, etc., and pointing out exactly what is meant by "baroque," "classic," "primitive," "picturesque," and other basic terms of art history and criticism. "A remarkable lesson in the art of seeing," SAT. REV. OF LITERATURE. Translated from the 7th German edition. 150 illus. 254pp. 6⅛ x 9¼. 20276-3 Paperbound $2.50

FOUNDATIONS OF MODERN ART, A. Ozenfant. Stimulating discussion of human creativity from paleolithic cave painting to modern painting, architecture, decorative arts. Fully illustrated with works of Gris, Lipchitz, Léger, Picasso, primitive, modern artifacts, architecture, industrial art, much more. 226 illustrations. 368pp. 6⅛ x 9¼. 20215-1 Paperbound $3.00

METALWORK AND ENAMELLING, H. Maryon. Probably the best book ever written on the subject. Tells everything necessary for the home manufacture of jewelry, rings, ear pendants, bowls, etc. Covers materials, tools, soldering, filigree, setting stones, raising patterns, repoussé work, damascening, niello, cloisonné, polishing, assaying, casting, and dozens of other techniques. The best substitute for apprenticeship to a master metalworker. 363 photos and figures. 374pp. 5½ x 8½. 22702-2 Paperbound $3.50

SHAKER FURNITURE, E. D. and F. Andrews. The most illuminating study of Shaker furniture ever written. Covers chronology, craftsmanship, houses, shops, etc. Includes over 200 photographs of chairs, tables, clocks, beds, benches, etc. "Mr. & Mrs. Andrews know all there is to know about Shaker furniture," Mark Van Doren, NATION. 48 full-page plates. 192pp. 7⅞ x 10¾. 20679-3 Paperbound $2.75

ANIMAL DRAWING: ANATOMY AND ACTION FOR ARTISTS, C. R. Knight. 158 studies, with full accompanying text, of such animals as the gorilla, bear, bison, dromedary, camel, vulture, pelican, iguana, shark, etc., by one of the greatest modern masters of animal drawing. Innumerable tips on how to get life expression into your work. "An excellent reference work," SAN FRANCISCO CHRONICLE. 158 illustrations. 156pp. 10½ x 8½. 20426-X Paperbound $3.00

Dover Books on Art

AFRICAN SCULPTURE, Ladislas Segy. 163 full-page plates illustrating masks, fertility figures, ceremonial objects, etc., of 50 West and Central African tribes—95% never before illustrated. 34-page introduction to African sculpture. "Mr. Segy is one of its top authorities," NEW YORKER. 164 full-page photographic plates. Introduction. Bibliography. 244pp. 6⅛ x 9¼.

20396-4 Paperbound $2.50

CALLIGRAPHY, J. G. Schwandner. First reprinting in 200 years of this legendary book of beautiful handwriting. Over 300 ornamental initials, 12 complete calligraphic alphabets, over 150 ornate frames and panels, 75 calligraphic pictures of cherubs, stags, lions, etc., thousands of flourishes, scrolls, etc., by the greatest 18th-century masters. All material can be copied or adapted without permission. Historical introduction. 158 full-page plates. 368pp. 9 x 13.

20475-8 Clothbound $12.50

A DIDEROT PICTORIAL ENCYCLOPEDIA OF TRADES AND INDUSTRY. Manufacturing and the Technical Arts in Plates Selected from "L'Encyclopédie ou Dictionnaire Raisonné des Sciences, des Arts, et des Métiers," of Denis Diderot, edited with text by C. Gillispie. Over 2000 illustrations on 485 full-page plates. Magnificent 18th-century engravings of men, women, and children working at such trades as milling flour, cheesemaking, charcoal burning, mining, silverplating, shoeing horses, making fine glass, printing, hundreds more, showing details of machinery, different steps in sequence, etc. A remarkable art work, but also the largest collection of working figures in print, copyright-free, for art directors, designers, etc. Two vols. 920pp. 9 x 12. Heavy library cloth.

22284-5, 22285-3 Two volume set $27.50

SILK SCREEN TECHNIQUES, J. Biegeleisen, M. Cohn. A practical step-by-step home course in one of the most versatile, least expensive graphic arts processes. How to build an inexpensive silk screen, prepare stencils, print, achieve special textures, use color, etc. Every step explained, diagrammed. 149 illustrations, 201pp. 6⅛ x 9¼.

20433-2 Paperbound $2.00

STICKS AND STONES, Lewis Mumford. An examination of forces influencing American architecture: the medieval tradition in early New England, the classical influence in Jefferson's time, the Brown Decades, the imperial facade, the machine age, etc. "A truly remarkable book," SAT. REV. OF LITERATURE. 2nd revised edition. 21 illus. xvii + 240pp. 5⅜ x 8.

20202-X Paperbound $2.00

Dover Books on Art

A HANDBOOK OF ANATOMY FOR ART STUDENTS, Arthur Thomson. This long-popular text teaches any student, regardless of level of technical competence, all the subtleties of human anatomy. Clear photographs, numerous line sketches and diagrams of bones, joints, etc. Use it as a text for home study, as a supplement to life class work, or as a lifelong sourcebook and reference volume. Author's prefaces. 67 plates, containing 40 line drawings, 86 photographs—mostly full page. 211 figures. Appendix. Index. xx + 459pp. 5⅜ x 8⅜. 21163-0 Paperbound $3.50

WHITTLING AND WOODCARVING, E. J. Tangerman. With this book, a beginner who is moderately handy can whittle or carve scores of useful objects, toys for children, gifts, or simply pass hours creatively and enjoyably. "Easy as well as instructive reading," N. Y. Herald Tribune Books. 464 illustrations, with appendix and index. x + 293pp. 5½ x 8⅛.
20965-2 Paperbound $2.00

ONE HUNDRED AND ONE PATCHWORK PATTERNS, Ruby Short McKim. Whether you have made a hundred quilts or none at all, you will find this the single most useful book on quiltmaking. There are 101 full patterns (all exact size) with full instructions for cutting and sewing. In addition there is some really choice folklore about the origin of the ingenious pattern names: "Monkey Wrench," "Road to California," "Drunkard's Path," "Crossed Canoes," to name a few. Over 500 illustrations. 124 pp. 7⅞ x 10¾. 20773-0 Paperbound $2.00

ART AND GEOMETRY, W. M. Ivins, Jr. Challenges the idea that the foundations of modern thought were laid in ancient Greece. Pitting Greek tactile-muscular intuitions of space against modern visual intuitions, the author, for 30 years curator of prints, Metropolitan Museum of Art, analyzes the differences between ancient and Renaissance painting and sculpture and tells of the first fruitful investigations of perspective. x + 113pp. 5⅜ x 8⅜. 20941-5 Paperbound $1.50

TEACH YOURSELF TO STUDY SCULPTURE, Wm. Gaunt. Useful details on the sculptor's art and craft, tools, carving and modeling; its relation to other arts; ways to look at sculpture; sculpture of the East and West; etc. "Useful both to the student and layman and a good refresher for the professional sculptor," Prof. J. Skeaping, Royal College of Art. 32 plates, 24 figures. Index. xii + 155pp. 7 x 4¼. 20976-8 Clothbound $2.50

Dover Books on Art

FOOT-HIGH LETTERS: A GUIDE TO LETTERING, M. Price.
28 15½ x 22½" plates, give classic Roman alphabet, one foot
high per letter, plus 9 other 2" high letter forms for each letter.
16 page syllabus. Ideal for lettering classes, home study. 28 plates
in box. 20239-9 $7.50

A HANDBOOK OF WEAVES, G. H. Oelsner. Most complete
book of weaves, fully explained, differentiated, illustrated. Plain
weaves, irregular, double-stitched, filling satins; derivative,
basket, rib weaves; steep, broken, herringbone, twills, lace, tricot,
many others. Translated, revised by S. S. Dale; supplement on
analysis of weaves. Bible for all handweavers. 1875 illustrations.
410pp. 6⅛ x 9¼. 20209-7 Clothbound $7.50

*JAPANESE HOMES AND THEIR SURROUNDINGS, E. S.
Morse.* Classic describes, analyses, illustrates all aspects of traditional Japanese home, from plan and structure to appoint-
ments, furniture, etc. Published in 1886, before Japanese architecture was contaminated by Western, this is strikingly modern
in beautiful, functional approach to living. Indispensable to every
architect, interior decorator, designer. 307 illustrations. Glossary.
410pp. 5⅝ x 8⅜. 20746-3 Paperbound $3.50

THE DRAWINGS OF HEINRICH KLEY. Uncut publication of
long-sought-after sketchbooks of satiric, ironic iconoclast. Remarkable fantasy, weird symbolism, brilliant technique make
Kley a shocking experience to layman, endless source of ideas,
techniques for artist. 200 drawings, original size, captions translated. Introduction. 136pp. 6 x 9. 20024-8 Paperbound $2.00

COSTUMES OF THE ANCIENTS, Thomas Hope. Beautiful,
clear, sharp line drawings of Greek and Roman figures in full
costume, by noted artist and antiquary of early 19th century.
Dress, armor, divinities, masks, etc. Invaluable sourcebook for
costumers, designers, first-rate picture file for illustrators, commercial artists. Introductory text by Hope. 300 plates. 6 x 9.
20021-3 Paperbound $2.50

VITRUVIUS: TEN BOOKS ON ARCHITECTURE. The most
influential book in the history of architecture. 1st century A.D.
Roman classic has influenced such men as Bramante, Palladio,
Michelangelo, up to present. Classic principles of design, harmony, etc. Fascinating reading. Definitive English translation by
Professor H. Morgan, Harvard. 344pp. 5⅜ x 8.
20645-9 Paperbound $3.00

THE STYLES OF ORNAMENT, A. Speltz. The largest collection of line ornament in print, with 3750 numbered illustrations arranged chronologically from Egypt, Assyria, Greeks, Romans, Etruscans, through Medieval, Renaissance, 18th century, and Victorian. No permissions, no fees needed to use or reproduce illustrations. 400 plates with 3750 illustrations. Bibliography. Index. 640pp. 6 x 9.   20577-6 Paperbound $3.00

THE ART OF ETCHING, E. S. Lumsden. Every step of the etching process from essential materials to completed proof is carefully and clearly explained, with 24 annotated plates exemplifying every technique and approach discussed. The book also features a rich survey of the art, with 105 annotated plates by masters. Invaluable for beginner to advanced etcher. 374pp. 5⅜ x 8.   20049-3 Paperbound $2.75

EPOCHS OF CHINESE AND JAPANESE ART, E. Fenollosa. Classic study of pre-20th century Oriental art, revealing, as does no other book, the important interrelationships between the art of China and Japan and their history and sociology. Illustrations include ancient bronzes, Buddhist paintings by Kobo Daishi, scroll paintings by Toba Sojo, prints by Nobusane, screens by Korin, woodcuts by Hokusai, Koryusai, Utamaro, Hiroshige and scores of other pieces by Chinese and Japanese masters. Biographical preface. Notes. Index. 242 illustrations. Total of lii + 439pp. plus 174 plates. 5⅝ x 8¼.
                    Two-volume set, 20364-6, 20365-4 Paperbound $5.00

OF THE JUST SHAPING OF LETTERS, Albrecht Dürer. This remarkable volume reveals Albrecht Dürer's rules for the geometric construction of Roman capitals and the formation of Gothic lower case and capital letters, complete with construction diagrams and directions. Of considerable practical interest to the contemporary illustrator, artist, and designer. Translated from the Latin text of the edition of 1535 by R. T. Nichol. Numerous letterform designs, construction diagrams, illustrations. iv + 43pp. 7⅞ x 10¾.   21306-4 Paperbound $1.25

DESIGN MOTIFS OF ANCIENT MEXICO, J. Enciso. Nearly 90% of these 766 superb designs from Aztec, Olmec, Totonac, Maya, and Toltec origins are unobtainable elsewhere. Contains plumed serpents, wind gods, animals, demons, dancers, monsters, etc. Excellent applied design source. Originally $17.50. 766 illustrations, thousands of motifs. 192pp. 6⅛ x 9¼.
                    20084-1 Paperbound $2.25

200 DECORATIVE TITLE-PAGES, edited by A. Nesbitt. Fascinating and informative from a historical point of view, this beautiful collection of decorated titles will be a great inspiration to students of design, commercial artists, advertising designers, etc. A complete survey of the genre from the first known decorated title to work in the first decades of this century. Bibliography and sources of the plates. 222pp. 8⅜ x 11¼.

21264-5 Paperbound $3.50

ON THE LAWS OF JAPANESE PAINTING, H. P. Bowie. This classic work on the philosophy and technique of Japanese art is based on the author's first-hand experiences studying art in Japan. Every aspect of Japanese painting is described: the use of the brush and other materials; laws governing conception and execution; subjects for Japanese paintings, etc. The best possible substitute for a series of lessons from a great Oriental master. Index. xv + 117pp. + 66 plates. 6⅛ x 9¼.

20030-2 Paperbound $2.50

PAINTING IN THE FAR EAST, L. Binyon. A study of over 1500 years of Oriental art by one of the world's outstanding authorities. The author chooses the most important masters in each period—Wu Tao-tzu, Toba Sojo, Kanaoka, Li Lung-mien, Masanobu, Okio, etc.—and examines the works, schools, and influence of each within their cultural context. 42 photographs. Sources of original works and selected bibliography. Notes including list of principal painters by periods. xx + 297pp. 6⅛ x 9¼.

20520-7 Paperbound $3.00

THE ALPHABET AND ELEMENTS OF LETTERING, F. W. Goudy. A beautifully illustrated volume on the aesthetics of letters and type faces and their history and development. Each plate consists of 15 forms of a single letter with the last plate devoted to the ampersand and the numerals. "A sound guide for all persons engaged in printing or drawing," Saturday Review. 27 full-page plates. 48 additional figures. xii + 131pp. 7⅞ x 10¾.

20792-7 Paperbound $2.25

PAINTING IN ISLAM, Sir Thomas W. Arnold. This scholarly study puts Islamic painting in its social and religious context and examines its relation to Islamic civilization in general. 65 full-page plates illustrate the text and give outstanding examples of Islamic art. 4 appendices. Index of mss. referred to. General Index. xxiv + 159pp. 6⅝ x 9¼.   21310-2 Paperbound $2.75